Across the Aisles

Sid Snyder's Remarkable Life in Groceries & Government

BY JEFF BURLINGAME
Edited by John C. Hughes

THE WASHINGTON STATE
HERITAGE CENTER

LEGACY PROJECT

Washington State Legislature

Oral History Program

First Edition
Copyright © 2013
Washington State Legacy Project
Office of the Secretary of State
All rights reserved.

ISBN 978-1-889320-28-1

Front cover photo: Louie Balukoff

Book design by Kathryn E. Campbell

Printed in the United States of America
by Gorham Printing, Centralia, Washington

This project is a partnership of the Secretary of State's Legacy Project,
the Washington State Heritage Center and the Legislative Oral History
Program. Special thanks to Tom Hoemann and Marty Brown.

For Lisa, Tierney and Grayson.

CONTENTS

Sid Snyder's 1997 resignation made front-page headlines in newspapers across the state, including the *Willapa Harbor Herald*, whose article was written by Jeff Burlingame, the author of Snyder's biography.

PROLOGUE

I T WAS MID-AFTERNOON on a typically blustery late-January day when Sid Snyder's phone rang. Outside the home's big windows, over the grassy dunes, the great gray Pacific rolled ashore on an empty Southwest Washington beach. Inside, seated at a table—and in the midst of the third of what would be dozens of lengthy interview sessions for this book—Sid decided to let the phone ring. Bette, standing in the kitchen and closer to the phone anyway, fielded the call in a matter-of-fact manner that suggested she had done this before.

"Sid's busy right now. Who is calling?"

It was a local woman with a concern. She needed Sid's help.

Yes, frequently to her chagrin, Bette *had* done this before. A decade earlier, when Sid was majority leader of the Washington State Senate, calls such as this were a daily occurrence—and not just one a day. "Got a problem? Call Sid!" was the mantra of those Sid had represented during his 50-some years of public service. He relished that reputation. Bette, well, sometimes not so much. "When I see people hanging on his every word and he deludes himself and gets that dedicated look, I smile politely, keep my evil thoughts to myself and descend into a trancelike state," she once wrote. "Sometimes my gag reflex kicks in, and I often feel justified to commit a selfish act or make a caustic comment—with careless disregard for his image. Of course, I am only fantasizing and I would never do that in word or deed, so I retain my subservient attitude and stand aside." Bette has a natural gift for satire— and the best satire is tinged with truth. Sid always said he would have been lost without her rudder. And her wry sense of humor.

Bette, anything but subservient, bit her tongue with this caller, too, politely offering to relay the message. She did so, also matter-of-factly.

The caller was troubled by the stance a lawmaker was taking on what she considered a crucial piece of legislation. She had a problem. She called Sid. "I'll make a call," Sid assured his wife. Later that day, he did. In a week, the legislation the caller hoped would pass passed. And the legislator in question voted for it, exactly what the caller had desired.

In most instances, assuming a causal relationship between Sid's call and the legislator's vote would be a stretch. But though he was 10 years removed from Olympia, Sid still wielded considerable power there. When he reached out, it meant something. This caller knew that. What the caller likely did not know—though perhaps she did—was that Sid had never truly left the Capitol behind. He may have visited less than a handful of times since his 2002 midterm resignation, but he still knew the game and its players. During the creation of this book, Sid consistently referred to the Legislature in the first person, as in "When *we* vote on the budget…" and "*Our* staff is fantastic." Asked about his choice of pronouns, Sid would offer, "I'm still there in spirit." Walk the marbled halls of the domed Legislative Building—mailing address: 416 Sid Snyder Avenue SW—and talk with the employees inside. When you do, it quickly becomes clear: Never were truer words spoken. "Gosh, I have a lot of great stories about Sid," an information clerk once told me. "Got a day or two?"

Sid's health steadily declined during the year we spent working on this book. Mark Twain once observed that "we" should be reserved for kings and people with tapeworms. But I say "we" because it is the pronoun that fits. Sid was always there, not just in spirit but as an active participant in this book's creation. He was well-prepared (and well-groomed!) for each interview session, and he always arrived with historical articles and photos he recently had uncovered. Most times, he also came with a mental list of people who needed to be called in order to capture his "complete" story. At least once during every visit I made to Long Beach, Bette would pull me aside and say, "I wish you would have known him in his prime." My reply never wavered: "I have known Sid for 15 years, and he is as sharp now as he was when I first met him." I was not just being polite. Even in his mid-80s, Sid could recall vital vote counts from 40 years earlier as effortlessly as most people recite nursery rhymes from their childhood. He also knew which way individual legislators had voted on those bills of import. "Be sure to check the *Journal* to see if I got that count right," he would say. I did what he told me to do, for a while at least. Then, after Sid had nailed several complicated and obscure particulars, I learned that lifting those heavy volumes off the State Library shelves was no longer necessary. Trusting Sid was easier, more enjoyable, and far less taxing on body and mind.

Those 15 years I had known Sid began with a baptism by fire. His headline-grabbing resignation in April 1997 occurred during my sixth day as a reporter at the weekly *Willapa Harbor Herald* in Raymond. Pacific County's newspaper of record also happened to be sited smack in the middle of Sid Country—the 19th Legislative District. The fear that ran through my beginner's mind when my boss pulled me aside first thing Monday morning and told me what Sid had done Saturday night—and that the story was mine—was enormous. I did not have to ask "Sid who?" but name recognition was about the extent of my knowledge of one of the state's most influential citizen-politicians. I spent most of the day readying questions before calling Sid at his grocery store. He was at the cash register, working a shift, seemingly unfazed that his resignation had been the lead story on TV news programs and headline material on the front page of every newspaper from Aberdeen to Vancouver. Or that some of those papers were on sale a few feet away from where he stood. "I'm 70 and my wife is 74," Sid told me. "There is life after the Senate."

Sid brought a copy of the resulting article to one of our earliest interviews for this book. "Angry Snyder quits Senate," read the above-the-fold headline. I was pleased, surprised—and more than a little relieved—to discover the story was error-free.

A diligent biographer strives to find someone who will say that his otherwise lionized subject was selfish, senseless, or a bona fide son of a bitch. Typically, this is an easy mission, especially if your subject was a high-ranking, party-line politician who spent a significant amount of time in the public eye. Then, uncovering disparagers is a slam dunk. But if your subject is a gentleman like Sid Snyder who celebrated civility, you can troll the political seas for dirt from sunup to sundown but you had better be sure to leave yourself enough time to stop by the grocery store to buy dinner on the way home. No matter how long your line was in the water, there will never be anything for the controversy griddle when you reel it in. I asked dozens of insiders and those closest to Sid—on the record and off—if they knew anybody who did not like him. "You might want to talk to such and such," a few said. "You know, he really made so and so mad when…," I heard from others. But, invariably, whatever had made Such and Such and So and So upset with Sid had washed away with time's tides. "That was no big deal," they would say. "Sid is a great guy." I did find mention of the occasional scandal that really wasn't, a darkhorse opponent slinging accusations, and several small-town letter writers who opposed the way Sid had handled an issue. Put any of those letter writers in a room with Sid for 30 minutes, I could not help but think, and they probably never would publicly call him out again. They still may not agree with Sid's vote, but they would know that it had come from the heart of a kind man who believed he had the best interests of his constituents in mind.

The reverence those constituents had for Sid hardly faded following his retirement, especially on the Long Beach Peninsula. "Thank you for all you've done for us, senator," was a constant refrain from locals when Sid and I were together in public. Sometimes, Sid would simply thank them right back. Other times he would say, "Please, call me Sid." The man, fondly referred to by many as the "governor of Southwest Washington," was far more humble than haughty, more aw-shucks head hanger than "look at me" limelight seeker. Sid loved the attention, but only because it meant he was serving well.

"Many legislative leaders, in order to do their jobs, keep members happy, and line up votes on issues, favor pragmatism over principle. Not Snyder," Rutgers University professor and state-government expert Alan Rosenthal wrote in the nationally circulated *State Government News* in 2002. "Snyder is a very different type of leader; he embodies the institution in which he serves. Whatever his ambitions, they do not involve exploiting the legislature, but rather caring for the legislature." Sid was especially proud of those words because the author was on the other side of the continent and had never met him.

My final in-person interview with Sid was conducted at his home on September 25, 2012. His mind was as sharp as ever. At the end of the interview, I sat down on the couch next to him, my feet carefully straddling the plastic line from his round-the-clock supply of oxygen, while Bette read him the first chapter of this book. I occasionally interrupted her to ask Sid for confirmation or clarification. When Bette finished, Sid diffidently acknowledged he liked the direction I was taking. Then I left him to write more.

"It was great to see you again, Sid."

"You, too, Jeff."

Sid died down the hall less than three weeks later, on October 14, just two days before I had hoped to return with a copy of the finished product. I regret not being able to share the entire book with him, but I also find comfort in knowing he did not need to hear it—because he helped create it.

How often do we tell our own life story? How often do we adjust, embellish, make sly cuts? And the longer life goes on, the fewer are those around to challenge our account, to remind us that our life is not our life, merely the story we have told about our life. Told to others, but—mainly—to ourselves.

—British author Julian Barnes

Folding chairs filled the scuffed gymnasium floor at Ilwaco High School during the day of Sid's memorial service. The Saturday-morning crowd—21 guest-book pages punctuated with household names—spilled into the surrounding bleachers. While waiting for the service to begin, attendees read the quotations in the program:

Sid was kind and gracious, and because he had the respect of everyone who knew him, he was able to bring people together to solve problems for the people of our state.

—United States Senator Patty Murray

Sid Snyder is one of the best examples I have ever known of how politics and public service, at their very best, can and should be conducted. His legacy will live on in the countless ways he changed our state and local communities and always for the better.

—Former United States Representative Brian Baird

Sid was the best legislative leader I ever served under. I would have followed him into hell [and] I would have been perfectly happy working under him at Sid's Market.

—Longtime state legislator Ken Jacobsen

Then they listened as his friends took to the podium:

Sid was that kind of leadership that was passed on from Scoop and Maggie. [He] then continued to do it the right way. When I started my federal career, he hosted a fundraiser for me at his downtown [Seattle] condo. I had no idea that Sid had a downtown condo. And then when I saw it, I thought, "That must be one heck of a supermarket." But that was Sid. He and Bette were the most generous people you ever met. We will all always, always remember the man from Southwest Washington and what he did for our state. And we will all, all try to emulate him in the future.

—United States Senator Maria Cantwell

Sid did come straight out of the soil of Washington state. He grew up poor in the Great Depression, and I believe that gave birth to, and explains, his generous spirit to those around him. To Sid Snyder, everyone he met deserved his quiet courtesy, his listening ear, and his respect. He was a true servant-leader. He knew that in order to get things done, in order to lead, he had to serve. And serve he did. More than half a century of long hours and long days. No one worked harder than Sid Snyder. Sid Snyder left the great state of Washington a far better place than when he found it. He did it through hard work, and he did it through humble determination.

—Governor Chris Gregoire

Sid professionalized the Senate staff, but he also instilled in that professional staff a respect, not just for the people we worked with and worked for, but he also instilled a respect for the institution. That is one of the things that will live with me for a long, long time. Sid was not a teacher; he was a mentor. Teachers have plans. Sid didn't have a plan. He just allowed us to watch his dedication, his respect, his innate ability to deal with people. His example was hard work, respect for others no matter what their position was in life, [and] love for all.

—Marty Brown, former director of the Office of Financial Management

Having a conversation with Sid was as comfortable as wearing an old pair of shoes. He had that ability to put you at ease, to focus completely on you, engage on you, and he acted in an absolute genuine manner. That's a lesson I learned from Sid Snyder.

—Nabiel Shawa, former Long Beach city administrator

There were many people who looked up to Sid Snyder as an adviser, mentor and good example of how to live and serve. I am one of them. Sid had an amazing work ethic. He was usually at the Capitol by 7 a.m. He would work as late as it took to get the job done. He would keep the Senate working until the midnight hour or later if that's what it took to meet the deadline. It always amazed me at how he had the energy to keep it up.

—Mark Doumit, former 19th District senator

Finally, they mourned with his eloquent only son:

Between the store and Olympia, Dad kept really busy. He didn't really take days off when my sisters and I were growing up. But when in town he was always home for a family dinner. And I always looked forward to the time before eating and after dinner before he returned to the store, when we would play catch and he would throw pop-ups and grounders to me. He set a tremendous example of how to live a life. He was honest, always honest. He didn't have to work at it. It was just the way he was. He did what needed to be done and did what was right without needing to think about it. He had integrity. The way he went about his work in Olympia is legendary. He favored pragmatism over a blind devotion to a certain ideology. He was unselfish. It wasn't self-deprecation, it was simply his way.

—Sid Snyder Jr.

Sitting through Sid's fittingly unassuming service, I remembered the brief online message Nirvana bassist Krist Novoselic had written when he learned of Sid's death: "All-around great human." I also thought of the eulogy Sid had delivered some 20 years earlier at the funeral of John Cherberg, the state's gregarious longtime lieutenant governor. I had found that five-page speech—dog-eared, handwritten and overflowing with scribbled-out words—earlier that week at the bottom of a cardboard box I had begun rummaging through the night of Sid's death. I kept thinking how the eulogy Sid had written for Cherberg eerily also could have been his own:

It isn't the longevity we remember. We remember [him] for the warm, caring person he was. When you think of the term "gentleman," you think of [him]. Always gracious, always kind, always available—he never turned anyone away. His office was open to one and all, and he made every visitor feel like the most important person he had ever welcomed. It didn't matter if you were the president, head of state, senior citizen, or a child. He gave—and therefore received—respect. He was an honorable man. He was proud of the Senate, and maintaining dignity was uppermost to him. He was tireless in his efforts to assist virtually thousands of citizens struggling to get through the obscure workings of state government or to aid in solving a personal problem. Not one person who sought assistance was turned away. [He] possessed a wonderful sense of humor and an amazing memory. And if he could find an audience of two or more, he would reminisce about the old legislative years, telling and retelling the same old stories.

To eschew hagiography, I believe a diligent biographer must make every effort to remain emotionally detached from his subject. I also believe in the words of Samuel Johnson, another wise British author: "Nobody can write the life of a man but those who have eat and drunk and lived in social intercourse with him." My goal was to apply both those philosophies to this book. I did, and quickly determined that when your subject is as affable as Sid Snyder, one or the other has to give. It is impossible to accomplish both.

The best thing about people who were so alive when they were alive is that when they are gone they are still here.

Jeff Burlingame
November 2012

Bob McCausland, *The Daily World*

One ▪ Hell in a Handbasket

No ONE WAS SURPRISED that talk of changing the rules is what set him off.

In fact, if anything about Sid Snyder's impassioned actions on the Washington State Senate floor on April 19, 1997, shocked anyone it was that the Democrat with a long-standing reputation for cross-aisle camaraderie was *capable* of being set off. But set off he was. Snyder was mad as hell. And, not unlike Peter Finch's brilliantly maniacal anchorman in the movie *Network*, he was not going to take this anymore.

Microphone wobbling in his right hand, left hand in the pocket of his trousers, the 70-year-old minority leader stood and faced the rostrum: "It seems like anytime that 25 people, after they've crashed and burned or the wheels come off, and they've dug a hell of a deep hole for themselves, they can't abide by the rules. They have to come in and change them. Rules are made so the majority can operate this place …"[1]

Snyder's head snapped to the back of the chamber. "… with the protection of the minority!" His face reddened. His head shook, jowls tagging along like visual exclamation points for whatever it was he was about to say. His voice swelled to a shout. "This is a travesty what you're doing today. It'll come back to haunt this body time and time again! I have a lot of respect for this place. But it's going to hell in a handbasket."[2]

The Republicans were the reason for Snyder's ire. Specifically, it was their desire to again vote on a $19 billion budget for the next biennium, 1997-1999—the same bill that had failed, been reconsidered, and had failed again. Century-old parliamentary procedure, at which Snyder was a master, declared the budget dead, but the Republicans wanted to modify that procedure—but only until the end of the year when the old rule would again take effect—and allow further reconsideration of the budget. Their goal was to hasten its passage. It was early evening of the 97th day of a 105-day session. Everyone was tired and wanted to go home, which would not happen without a budget.

Majority Leader Dan McDonald was the subject of Snyder's gaze. The accomplished engineer and veteran lawmaker from Yarrow Point on the east side of Lake Washington knew that was the case. He picked up his microphone, and calmly countered: "Rules are meant to drive us to conclusion. That's exactly what we need to do. It is not as if the suspension of rules or the amendment of rules is a new thing. It has been done before; it will be done in the future. We are trying to drive to conclusion of the will of the Legislature with respect to the budget. This expedites that process. It makes it clear. It makes it concise. It makes it done by today."[3]

After several minutes of back and forth, the proposal to change the rules passed along party lines. In his first session as Senate president, Lieutenant Governor Brad Owen ruled the budget bill could be reconsidered again. The Democrat from Shelton, who just a year earlier had served in the Senate alongside Snyder and McDonald, said he was doing so reluctantly: "The changes accomplished here today attack the fundamental integrity by changing a basic understanding of parliamentary procedure which the president relied on yesterday in ruling on [the budget bill]. The wisdom of a rule which prohibits endless reconsideration was clearly explained by Thomas Reed more than 100 years ago. The president fears that this change will have long-standing repercussions."[4]

His face spotlighted by flashbulbs, Snyder took Owen's frustration a step further. Once again, he picked up his microphone: "I, too, am highly disappointed in the actions of this body in the last few minutes. I've always been very proud to be associated with this Senate and previous to that, the House of Representatives. I feel that my voice and my vote have been very diminished. And I'm going to immediately submit my resignation as a senator to the 19th District to the governor."[5]

Snyder dropped the microphone and, still seething, made his way from the chamber. Rosa Franklin, a Tacoma Democrat, was clearly shaken. "This should not have happened. This should not have happened!" she told the Republicans. "Look what is happening. You have divided us."[6]

Three minutes later, the budget bill passed, 26-0. Twenty-two Democrats had followed their leader off the floor. Some—including Senators Adam Kline and Mary Margaret Haugen—even followed him to his car in the Capitol basement, pleading with him to stay. Snyder refused. He had spent a decade helping teach a class on parliamentary procedure to freshman House members. He had served 19 years as secretary of the Senate, the body's chief parliamentarian. He knew the rules, believed in them, and over the years had grown frustrated as he watched their significance erode. Changing the rules to speed something up was disrespectful. The integrity of the institution he had served for the past 48 years had been damaged.

Snyder pulled out of the basement in his burgundy Cadillac, the one in which he routinely covered 35,000 miles a year, swinging from meeting to meeting across his sprawling district in Southwest Washington. He headed for the highway via the Olympia street that one day would bear his name, dialed home on his car phone, and told his shocked wife he would be there in two hours: *Yes, dear, I know I've teased you with this in the past. This time it is for good.*

He drove through the Black Hills, descended into Elma and passed the blinking warning lights atop the mothballed cooling towers he would help turn into a prosperous business park. As he drove on into the night, he fielded phone calls from the governor and a congressman. Finally, he shut off his phone. In silence now, he cut through the town of Montesano, where he and Bette Kennedy had arrived 46 years before in a barely running Plymouth to sign their marriage license. Seventy miles later, he passed the small-town market and flagship bank branch that had helped hoist him from Depression-era welfare child to self-made millionaire. He passed another street that one day would bear his name, then the above-store apartment where his wedding ceremony had taken place, sans photograph because superfluity was not in the budget.

Then he was home. He thought he would never again make the 110-mile trek to the Capitol, his home away from home for so many years. That decision was not based upon *Reed's Parliamentary Rules*; it was based upon life's rules. Sid Snyder never broke the rules.

Two ▪ Little Chicago

THE ALLEN STREET BRIDGE had its glory days, but not many of them.

Built in 1906 to replace a year-old span that had washed away in a flood, the two-lane drawbridge was a 600-foot-long manufacturing marvel. It featured a counterbalanced suspension system that raised two narrow wooden decks to allow boats to continue their voyage up or down the Cowlitz River, and then lowered them so cars, pedestrians, and horse-drawn wagons could continue their journeys over the only direct link between the towns of Kelso and Catlin.

Beauty though it was, the $25,000 wooden span quickly proved no better than those before it when pitted against the soggy Southwest Washington weather. Within five years, several of its rotten planks had been topped with new ones. By 1920, moisture had rendered the bridge so rickety that the most cautious locals refused to use it. Others crossed it reluctantly. Plans were made to construct another bridge slightly downriver—this time out of steel.[1]

Construction of the new bridge was all but finished on January 3, 1923, when a perfect storm struck the old one. Recent heavy rains had waterlogged its planks, which in many spots were now two or three deep. A massive logjam in the river below pounded its piers. During an evening shift change at the Long-Bell Lumber Company, a stalled vehicle backed up traffic across the span. Now it was supporting a line of cars, pedestrians, and at least one team of wagon-hauling horses. Under the stress of it all, a steel suspension cable snapped. The bridge's supporting towers and entire middle span—and every vehicle, person, and quadruped on it—plunged into the cold and muddy Cowlitz. Dozens of people were trapped underneath the broken bridge section, which had been flipped by the current the moment it hit the water.

R.H. Oswalt, a Long-Bell worker on foot, was one of those trapped. "Timbers fell and crashed about me," he said, broken-armed and bandaged, from his hospital bed a day later. "I was carried to the bottom by the fallen wreckage, but how long I was under water I cannot say. I fought my way to the surface but the timbers rolled about and over me as I struggled to climb them. I was pinned between two timbers and expected to be crushed to death."[2]

The logs Oswalt were pinned between drifted to the new bridge. He was pinioned there just long enough for an unidentified hero to reach over the side of a boat and hoist him to safety. Other survivors shared similar stories. Some swam or floated atop debris until they were plucked from the water or somehow scrambled up the muddy river banks to shore. Many of those riding in cars never got their doors open before they sank to the bottom. W.M. Sullivan, who had both legs crushed in the disaster, said that just before he was rescued by a boat he had heard cries for help coming from those trapped inside two sinking cars.[3] Others were swept two miles downstream to the Columbia River, and never seen again.

The official tally listed 17 people killed, though witnesses believed two times that number was more accurate. Among the dead were a Cowlitz County commissioner-elect, several Long-Bell workers, 58-year-old Kelso pioneer Alonzo Grant Huntington, his wife, and their adult son. Had the collapse occurred minutes earlier, more people surely would have been killed. A work crew repairing the bridge had just gone home for the day. As it was, the Allen Street Bridge collapse was the deadliest such accident in Washington history, and it led to the creation of the state's bridge inspection program.

Edwin Alfonso "Fonny" Snyder arrived in Kelso the following day, as cranes were hoisting cars from the Cowlitz and divers searched for bodies. The entire city of Kelso "was in a wild tumult … [and] those apprehensive of safety of relatives or friends rushed madly from hospital to hospital and back to the bank of the river."[4] The 53-year-old former hackney driver from Kalamazoo, Michigan, was passing through on his way to Astoria, Oregon, where he planned to discuss job prospects with a brother who was working as a dairy farmer. Fonny never made it across the Columbia.

His journey had begun in Douglas County, a Central Washington wheat-growing region so deeply affected by drought and the Depression that nearly 2,000 of its 9,300 residents would flee in search of greener pastures during the 1920s. For a man who made a living cutting hair—a spinoff from the sheep-shearing he had done as a youth—a population in decline was not a good thing. So when Fonny Snyder heard the faint sound of opportunity knocking west of the Cascades, he followed. When he arrived in Cowlitz County, in spite of the bridge-related tumult, he saw gold at the end of that sonic rainbow. Cowlitz County was in the midst of a decade-long population explosion that eventually tripled its Census count to 32,000. When Fonny reached Kelso, signs of that growth were everywhere. Timber was one reason. Kansas City businessman Robert Alexander Long was another. A year earlier, Long had decided to expand his lumber empire west after his company had clear-cut most of its hold-ings in the South. Long's ambitions were boundless. He had wanted to build what would be the largest lumber mill in the world at the confluence of the Columbia and Cowlitz rivers.

Kelso residents were ecstatic. That is, until they learned it would not be their city in which the anticipated thousands of workers would be resid-ing and spending money. For Long wanted to build more than a sawmill. He wanted to build a large "planned city" around his mill, one that would dwarf gritty Kelso in both size and grandeur. And that is exactly what he did. Longview—named after its founder's farm in Missouri—was dedicated in July 1923, and incorporated the following year. Frank Dallam Jr., the publisher of Kelso's *Daily Tribune* who had served as secretary to Washington governors Albert Mead and Marion Hay and also as secretary of the Senate wrote that, over time, the initial good will between Kelso and Long's people had given way to "ever increasing resentments of what are interpreted and believed to be evidences of determination…to dominate not only the city they have built, but the entire region over which the influence of their organization can extend."[5] Thus began an intense rivalry between Longview and Kelso that still exists today.

Fonny Snyder had no allegiances to either faction. But, like many men at the time, he saw hope amid the buzz. So much so that he sent for his family—his wife, Adahlena, 14-year-old Floyd Edwin, 12-year-old Victor Wellington, and 9-month-old Rufus William—and leased a corner building on Kelso's busy West Main Street. There, he opened a barbershop.

Fonny and Adahlena Beeman Snyder—Adah for short—now 39, had married in 1906 in Lewiston, Idaho, less than 20 miles from the tiny Palouse burg of Genesee where Adah had been born on April 19, 1883. Thanks to several generations of genealogically astute Beeman descendants, substantially more is known about Adah's family history than her husband's. The family has definitively traced its lineage to Thomas Beeman, a one-time real estate dabbler from Eastern Connecticut who married in 1712, fathered several children, and then in the 1730s marched his family west across the Connecticut River in search of enough land to provide for his family. The Beemans landed alongside the rugged, virgin wilderness near the Housatonic River, at today's border with New York. There, Thomas Beeman became a landholder of the colonial town of Kent. He paid 185 pounds sterling for 1,000 acres of the 50,000-acre town, and acquired more land over the next decade, some of which he sold to his male progeny "for diverse good cause and good considerations … but more for parential [sic] love and affection that I have for my sons."[6]

Beeman's pioneering spirit trickled through his bloodline to Adah's father, Rufus Horatio Beeman, who left home at 12 to work in the Wisconsin mines. In 1852, now 19, Rufus set out across the plains to Oregon. At 22, he "fought the savages" and was nearly killed saving an injured comrade at the bloody Battle of Hungry Hill during the Rogue River Indian War. During the middle of that nine-month conflict, Rufus married Caroline McBee at Roseburg, Oregon, two days after her 14th birthday.[7]

Exactly what drew the pair together is unknown, although they did share much in common despite an eight-year age gap. Caroline also had crossed the Plains in 1852 for "the riches and wonders of far-away Willamette."[8] The 10-year-old and her extended family had begun their

Rufus Horatio Beeman, Sid Snyder's grandfather, was an active Democrat born in Pennsylvania who, in the 1880s, ran for sheriff of Nez Perce County, Idaho. He lost the election by one vote.
An Illustrated History of North Idaho

expedition April 1 in Ray County, Missouri. Caroline's parents, Levi and Elizabeth, contracted cholera near present-day Nebraska, and shortly thereafter were "sleeping the sleep that knows no waking upon this earth."[9] Their grieving family pushed on. Caroline lost two siblings along the way, but she and the rest of her group finally made it to the eastern slopes of the Cascade Mountains six months after they had begun. They wintered there, then separated, with Caroline landing in Portland in the spring of 1853. Years later, in an oral history she dictated to a grandson, Victor Snyder, Caroline described the Portland she first saw as "a typical frontier town [with] one main street that ran along the Willamette River. It had a few stores, and plenty of saloons and gambling halls. The timber grew very near the water's edge and as soon as a little space was cleared off a new house would go up in this spot."[10] Her school, she said, was taught by a woman who "it would not have taken a very smart person to be as intelligent as she."[11]

Caroline and Rufus moved to Walla Walla in 1861, where Rufus worked as a miner, farmer, and "freighter." In 1874, the couple moved to Genesee, where Rufus—a medium-built man with gray eyes, black hair and a devilish goatee—operated a general store and ran for sheriff of Nez Perce County, losing by one vote. He was a man so noteworthy that, according to *An Illustrated History of North Idaho*, even President Theodore Roosevelt would have been impressed by him had they ever met. "Mr. Beeman was an active Democrat in earlier days, but is not so much now," the book noted. "He is a respected and prominent man in this community."[12] Adah Beeman, Sid Snyder's mother, was the 13th of 14 children born to Rufus and Caroline.

Fonny Snyder had earned respect as a barber, but it would be a stretch to label him as prominent by the time his fourth son, Sidney Robert, was born July 30, 1926, in Kelso. At that time, Fonny and Adah had seen 100 years of life between them—he 57, she 43—and were living in a small home on South 4th Avenue, 1,000 feet east of the dikeless, flood-prone Cowlitz River. It was barely three miles from the Columbia, in an area of the state where Mother Nature was particularly harsh on homes and country. Seventy-five years earlier, the marshy land surrounding the Snyder home had been a grazing area for Hudson's Bay Company cattle. One hundred years earlier, it had been hunting ground for the Cowlitz and Chinook Indians. It was fertile. And wet.

Fonny suffered from diabetes, and his health steadily declined as he entered his 60s. At 62, he suffered a stroke and died at home shortly thereafter, on November 1, 1931, surrounded by family. Five-year-old Sid would live the rest of his life with only one sad memory of his father: "The only thing I can remember is going by the casket and my mother patting him on the face. I never knew anybody that I called Dad."

After Fonny's death, Adah's two oldest sons stepped up to help provide. The eldest, Floyd, took over his father's barbershop. Then, after he married on New Year's Day 1933, he moved his bride into the cramped Snyder home. Vic—who nearly died of pneumonia as an infant and suffered with weak lungs his entire life—joined the New Deal's Civilian

Conservation Corps after high school. He was sent to Yacolt in nearby Clark County, where he felled bug-infested snags left behind from a massive 1902 fire that had killed 38 people and wiped out 238,000 acres of prime timberland. Vic earned $30 a month for his efforts, and sent $25 of it home to his family. Over the years, Sid's big brothers also had their fill of turns rising before dawn and walking the four miles across the Allen Street Bridge to Longview's hiring hall, hoping to make 20 cents an hour filling in for a day at whatever mill might need them.

Pushing 50 and in the midst of the Great Depression, Adah Snyder was forced to get creative. She grew apples and vegetables, raised chickens and rabbits, took in boarders, and hand-washed laundry for the area's many bachelor teachers, most of whom were staying in area rooming houses. The Snyders' most noteworthy lodger was James Butler, brother of future Congresswoman Julia Butler Hansen. He taught in Cowlitz County before leaving for Los Angeles and a job as head of the Drama Department at the University of Southern California.

For her frugality, Adah earned the nickname "Grandma Ikey." It was a term tinged with anti-Semitism, but to the Snyders it was endearing and

PAGE FIVE

EDWIN SNYDER DIES AT HOME

West Side Barber Will Be Buried Here Tuesday Morning

Edwin A. Snyder, aged 62 years, died at the family home in Kelso, 1405 South Fourth avenue, Sunday evening after a short illness. Although he had not been in the best of health for some time his serious illness was brief. He was a barber by trade and operated a shop in West Kelso.

The family came here about eight years ago. For a long time they lived in Idaho. He is survived by the widow, Adah Snyder, and four sons, Floyd, Victor, Rufus and Robert. There are also four brothers.

Funeral services will be held at the Nat R. Smith funeral chapel at 10:00 o'clock Tuesday morning. Rev. R. C. Barnes of the Central Christian church will officiate. Burial will be in the I. O. O. F. cemetery.

Sid Snyder was five years old when his father, Edwin Alfonso "Fonny" Snyder, died on November 1, 1931, at age 62. Fonny's obituary was published the following day in *The (Kelso) Daily Tribune*.

stood simply for the thriftiness their mom was forced to exhibit. Young Sid—known by those close to him as Bob or Bobby throughout his child-hood—did his part too, towing his old red wagon around the neighbor-hood, selling home-grown apples, vegetables and rabbits, and delivering the laundry his mom had cleaned. "We got by," he said. "We didn't know we were in a depression. Everybody was poor. I had one pair of shoes, and we got them half-soled when the socks started to show through the bottom. There were a few rich people over in Longview that lived along the lake, and they were probably officials with Long-Bell."

Thanksgiving dinner at the Snyder home never centered on a turkey. The family would snatch a rooster from the yard, chop off its head, stuff it, and bake and carve it as if it were the more expensive bird. Though strug-gling, the family still passed on to others whatever blessings it could, mostly through the Nazarene church one block over, where Sid attended Sunday school. "Yes, things were tough," Sid recalled. "But one thing that almost always brings tears to my eyes is thinking about Christmastime, when the church always rallied around and you got an orange in your stocking and so forth. They would ask if anyone could donate a dollar for the money for these stockings, then ask who could donate 50 cents. And my mother said, 'We can give 50 cents.' And I was so proud we could do our part."

Remaining on their feet throughout the Depression was difficult enough, but the Snyders also absorbed staggering blows from Mother Nature. The first occurred on June 15, 1933, when a "100-year flood" hit the Cowlitz River. At noon that day, the Coweeman River dike broke, inun-dating South Kelso and covering many homes to their eaves. The Snyders lived far enough away to avoid the brunt of the flood, but hundreds of their neighbors were forced to evacuate empty-handed. The displaced families included the Jankes, whose 6-year-old daughter, Rose, later recalled seeing "an eight-foot wall of water" coming toward her home. "Mill whistles blew. Sirens blew," she said. "Everyone was aware that the dike had broke and people were there almost immediately with trucks to evacuate us."[13] Many Kelso families were allowed to live in vacant Long-Bell homes across the

Cowlitz until the water receded. The seven-member Janke family ended up sharing a two-story Victorian house with 13 others. They were not able to return to their own house until September.

Half a year later, a few days before Christmas, came another disaster. This *was* the 100-year-flood. The Cowlitz, the Coweeman and many other rivers and streams in Southwest Washington surged over their banks. In many spots, the flood was the largest ever recorded. Sid, 7 years old at the time, recalled water rushing down his street and through his neighborhood. He now knew how Rose Janke felt. Once again, homes were flooded to their eaves and families evacuated on a moment's notice. The Red Cross was called in to distribute clothing, and the Kelso Methodist Church was turned into a makeshift soup kitchen that fed hundreds. Damage was in the millions. The Snyders were forced to evacuate to a hill near the high school for a couple of days. The flood's impact could be seen across the region for months. "We had a hen that hatched duck eggs," Sid joked.

The Snyders persevered, and as the alphabet-soup programs of Franklin D. Roosevelt's New Deal began to alleviate some of the Depression's hardships across the nation, Sid started doing more to ease his family's distress by taking a dollar-a-week job doing "flunky work" at Kreiger's Corner market on South Pacific Avenue, four blocks from home. He was 12 when he started working for Fred Kreiger, a German butcher, a few hours each day after school, all day Saturday and until the store closed at noon on Sunday. In addition to his pay, he received discounts. For 25 cents, he could buy enough round steak to feed everyone in the house—for one good meal at least. "There were 60 kids in the neighborhood that envied me because I had a job. I think the reason I got the job was that my mother was a widow."

Regardless of the rationale Fred Kreiger had used to select Sid as his do-everything helper, it was immediately obvious he and his wife, May, had made the right selection. Sid proved a hard worker and practically became part of the Kreiger family. On Sunday afternoons in the summer, after closing the store, Fred and Sid would hop into Fred's Packard coupe and hit the scenic Columbia River Highway for Vaughn Street Park in

Portland to watch the Portland Beavers play Pacific Coast League baseball. The fact that the Beavers were dreadful did not matter to Sid. He enjoyed every minute of the Sunday doubleheaders, delighted to see in person the players whose names he knew by heart from listening to the store's radio each evening.

Sid's Saturdays were not as enjoyable, but equally educational. After Kreiger's closed for the day, he hiked across town to West Kelso to mop and wax the floors of his brother's barbershop. It was there, on brothel-heavy, tavern-filled West Main Street, that Sid learned the reason his hometown had long been known as "Little Chicago." A lot of the loggers who lived in camps around the county came into town by train on Friday nights, Sid recalled. "There used to be some pretty good brawls on the streets. There were lots of houses of ill repute. It was a rough-and-tumble town."

The Snyders did not have indoor plumbing until Sid was a sopho- more in high school, which was the same year Japanese fighter planes attacked Pearl Harbor and brought America formally into World War II. Sid

Kreiger's Corner store is shown here in the mid-1920s, shortly after it was constructed. Snyder began working at the store in 1938, when he was 12 years old. He worked seven days a week for a dollar. *Courtesy Sally McNulty*

was spending part of his only afternoon off at a Kelso ice cream parlor when he heard the news on December 7, 1941, a day, FDR said, "which will live in infamy." His first reaction was the same as that of most Americans, particularly teenagers in small towns who were worried more about sustenance than geography:

"Where's Pearl Harbor?"

He quickly found out.

"The next day the recruiting offices were just flooded with people joining the service," Sid said. "I can remember listening

Sid as a boy. *Snyder family photo*

to President Roosevelt's speech over the loudspeaker we had in Mister [Richard] Sloat's class." FDR's patrician voice was familiar to millions. Sid had grown up Democrat—"most everybody was in those days"—listening to the president's "Fireside Chats." Walter Winchell's gossip-filled Sunday night broadcast was another time when they crowded around his family's second-hand radio. FDR's declaration that "with confidence in our armed forces—with the unbounding determination of our people—we will gain the inevitable triumph, so help us God," sparked intense patriotism in Kelso and all across the country. Sid's teacher, Mister Sloat, signed up for the Marines. He was killed in action a short time later.

Not yet old enough to enlist, Sid quit his job at Kreiger's—which now earned him $10 a week—to work at a service station that had lost most its employees to the military. He pumped gas 10 hours a day, six days a week, and made $18 for his efforts, but was forced to leave the job when high school resumed in the fall. He found a job at the Long-Bell mill that did not conflict with his classes, but cost him any hope of quality sleep.

The Snyder boys dress up for a family portrait in the 1940s. Sid is seated at the bottom, and surrounded by, from left to right, Floyd, Rufus, and Vic. *Snyder family photo*

For 95 cents an hour, Sid stacked lumber by hand for the dry kiln from 6 p.m. to 2:40 a.m. each weekday, slept a few hours, and then went to school. Somehow he maintained the same reasonable marks he had since his earliest grade-school days. Despite a steel-trap mind, Sid never was a scholar. With his hardscrabble life, it was not difficult to understand why.

"At Wallace Grade School, they had two classes. They had one for the brightest 30 kids and one for the dumbest 30 kids. I went from the dumbest to the brightest, from the top of the dumb kids to the bottom of the bright kids," he said years later with a chuckle. Math was his best subject.

Working was Sid's extra-curricular activity of necessity throughout his school years, although he did try out for football his junior year. A heart murmur discovered during a routine physical ended his playing days before they began. His job at Long-Bell soon ended, too, when snowfall halted the company's logging operations. The overnight shift was temporarily curtailed. Brother Vic, who worked in the office at Reynolds Metal in Longview, got Sid a job punching aluminum pots on the graveyard shift until Long-Bell reinstituted its night shift come spring. The summer before his senior year, Sid fought forest fires for the state. That fall, he returned to work at Long-Bell.

Sid's jobs all were vital to keeping the family afloat, although World War II also provided opportunities for women to work outside the home for the first time. Sid's mother, 60 and crippled with arthritis, began carpooling daily to Vancouver to sit on a bucket at the Kaiser Shipyard and scrape rust from metal used to build cargo-carrying Liberty ships for the Navy. It was grueling work for a healthy man, let alone an older woman in her condition. "She never complained, never at all, about her lot in life," Sid said. "She had a good sense of humor, and she was always proud of her kids and what they accomplished. Growing up under the circumstances that she had, she thought if we could get a good job at one of those lumber mills, that would be the ultimate in life. Education wasn't really stressed. Just get out and get a job and go to work."

A mother-pleasing mill career is likely what Snyder would have had, had World War II not occurred. War changed young men's goals across the United States, including Sid's. "All we had to look forward to as males in high school was to go into the service when you got out of school." That is exactly what he did after graduating from Kelso High in June 1944. A few months prior to graduation, Sid had traveled with his friend Don Morris to

Portland so Don could take the Army Air Force's entrance exam. Though he was only 17, Sid decided to take the test, too. The Army was his branch of choice, mainly because his brothers Floyd and Rufus were in it. He also knew that by selecting a branch prior to his 18th birthday he could avoid being drafted and stood a good chance of getting his branch of choice. "The next thing I knew," Sid said, "I raised my hand and was sworn in with the idea that I'd be called right after I turned 18."

The tide of the war had changed dramatically by the time Snyder turned 18 on July 30, 1944. The Army Air Force no longer needed new mechanics or flight crews, so Snyder did not get the call until January 1945. He was sent to basic training in Biloxi, Mississippi, and took a flight-school test. At the beginning of the war, two-thirds of those who took the test qualified to be pilots, but by the time Snyder took it, entry into the program had become stricter. Snyder made the cut, but there was no school open for him to attend. Instead, he ended up in Yuma, Arizona, where the barracks were "just two-by-fours with drywall on top of them and there was no air conditioning." Snyder's job, one of the best on base given the conditions, was guarding the water tower.

Snyder's stint in the Army Air Force began in January 1945 and ended that November. He is shown here in Yuma, Arizona, where his main duty was to guard the base's water tower. *Snyder family photo*

When the war ended in August, Snyder was sent back to Biloxi for radio-operator training. "We got back there and they said, 'Hell, we don't need mechanics *or* radio men. If you want to join, you

Snyder, far right, stands with three of his fellow GIs—from left, Smalling, Smith, and Wiltnup—on base in Yuma. *Snyder family photo*

can be part of the occupational force, or you can get out,' " Snyder said. "I chose to get out." Snyder was discharged on November 15, 1945. His military career lasted nine months and 29 days. "I was the last to leave for the war and the first to be sent home," he said.

None of the Snyder brothers ever made it overseas, but Sid still witnessed the impact serving in horrific conditions had on others. "I had friends who spent three years in the jungles over in New Guinea," he said. When one of those friends, after returning, acted a little strange sometimes, Sid would defend him to others. He would say, "Well, I think it's because he spent three years in the jungle and saw a lot of his buddies get cut in two with machine gun fire. How can you not?" Others who had served would go on drinking sprees. "Some of my classmates were killed and ones that were a year or two ahead of me were killed. I never forgot those things."

Snyder attended Lower Columbia Community College in Longview during the winter and spring quarters in 1946. That summer, he toyed with the idea of transferring to the just-opened Olympic Community College in Bremerton, the wartime boom town. Then, mostly on a whim, he and a few friends hit the highway and headed west. They landed in a sleepy coastal town near where the mighty Columbia rolls on into the mightier Pacific, just north of the spot where some 141 years earlier Meriwether Lewis and William Clark had experienced "great joy" when the "ocian" first came into view. The 20-year-old Snyder fell in love with everything about the town, even its near-constant drizzle. He called it Oregon mist, as in it had *missed* Oregon and hit Washington. He would never leave. "I never had enough money to. And when I did, I didn't want to." It was always nice at the beach, he had discovered. And some days were even nicer.

Three ▪ Bette

Someday I'll no doubt meet a man
To whom I'll want to wed
But it's a cinch he'll never marry me
In the condition I crawl in bed.
For I'm a hideous sight each night
From my toes up to my head
I'm enough to scare children and even ghosts
When I get ready for bed.

From "Life is Hard—Especially for a Bride" by Bette Kennedy, 1946

SASSY, ATTRACTIVE, and free-spirited, with Fifth Avenue tastes and Wall Street confidence, Bette Kennedy was the kind of woman lesser men feared and smarter men fought for when she strode into the Long Beach Tavern one summer evening in 1950. Up from Southern California with a girl-friend to visit family, the leggy 27-year-old brunette had just closed shop on all the action the fishing hamlet of Ilwaco had to offer—that action being at her family's tavern—so she decided to head five minutes up the coast in search of a lively dance floor. She found one in Long Beach, and danced the night away to Wurlitzer music with a young local named Merrill Bailey, while her friend intermittently paired off with a 24-year-old bingo caller with two left feet named Sid Snyder.

Although the "Kelso Two-Step"—Bette's name for Sid's gauche dance moves—had not appealed to her in the least, she gave in when Sid asked her at the end of the night if she would go out with him the next day.

"I thought, 'Oh, boy, this kid's got some future. He's got a nice car,' " she recalled. "And here later I found out he had borrowed it. He didn't even own a car!" Her suitor did not have a home, either, at least not a permanent one. When Bette Kennedy met him, Sid was living just up the road from the tavern in a $3.50-a-night room at the Balboa Motor Hotel.

Snyder had two strikes against him, but he also had something many of the California players Bette Kennedy had been dating did not: depth. At the end of their

Bette did some photo sessions during her days in California, including this one on the steps of a hotel. *Snyder family photo*

long drive down the beach in a borrowed Ford, she found herself impressed with all the small-town boy had to offer. "He was so personable, and everybody liked him. It didn't matter old or young. And he knew everybody's birthday in the county, I think. A word for him would just be 'nice.' " Snyder thought his California girl was the whole package—"She was the best looking. Easy to get along with. Bright, no question about that, with a good sense of humor. I guess it was kind of love at first sight."

The couple's long drives on the beach in a borrowed car progressed into longer walks on the beach on borrowed time. Nights at the Long Beach Tavern were spent holding hands, talking, and, yes, dancing the Kelso Two-Step. When the time came to return to California, Bette wanted to stay. She had her belongings shipped to her, and took a leap of faith, one of several she had taken in her lifetime. This time, if romance proved fickle, as it had before, at least she was back home, surrounded by family to slow her fall.

Risks never frightened Betty Ann Kennedy, an independent girl who as a teen changed the spelling of her first name in homage to the sloe-eyed actress, Bette Davis. She was born 50 miles northeast of Long Beach in Willapa, a once-booming logging town, on March 28, 1923. Her childhood had been punctuated with many of the same Depression-fueled hardships as Snyder's, minus the thorny task of managing it all with a single parent at the helm.

Kennedy's hometown was situated at the spot where the Willapa River deepened on its journey from the rolling evergreen Willapa Hills to the Pacific Ocean. It was the perfect place to load logs and lumber for trans-port to markets up and down the coast. That prime location made Willapa the hub of the valley beginning in the 1870s. At one point in the latter part of the century, it was home to three hotels, several saloons, and the *Willapa Republican*, a weekly run by lawyer F.L. Putney, who had served two years in Washington's early House of Representatives.

Willapa's heyday had passed by the time Bette Kennedy was born. Downriver towns, Raymond and South Bend, had stolen away jobs and resi-dents. The men who remained in Willapa generally worked in nearby logging camps while their wives raised families and tended to small gardens and any

Bette, at the time "Betty," as a young child in Willapa. *Snyder family photo*

livestock the family was fortunate enough to have acquired. That is precisely what Bette's parents, Ala and Ethel Kennedy, did. She and her two
older siblings—Jim and Evelyn—helped with the housework and other
chores, milking the family's lone cow once a day. Their father logged until
he was too old to do so, then moved on to a night watchman's job at a
lumber mill. During the day, he picked berries and peeled cascara bark
to help pay for his children's school clothes. It was a meager tiny-town
existence but there were benefits to be had, too. At Willapa, for example,
no one locked their doors.

Music was a staple in the Kennedy home. Many evenings would be
filled with Evelyn playing piano as Jim and Bette sang along to current hits
such as "Side by Side," a love song so popular that nearly a dozen artists
released recordings of it in 1927 alone.

It was when she hit high school that Bette changed the spelling of
her first name as a tribute to Bette Davis. The Willapa Bette bore more
than a passing resemblance to the movie star, too. At 5-foot-7, she stood
four inches taller, but they both had large, hypnotizing eyes. To her dis-
may, however, Bette Kennedy was rail-thin, while the other Bette was slim
but curvy. Skinny was not in vogue at the time, so her mother plopped
whipping cream atop a cup of hot chocolate every night and made her
drink it in hopes of fattening her up. It did not work. Part of the reason
was how active she was. Bette played in the high school band and was a
cheerleader. On Fridays, she would drop Dad off at work at 4 p.m., put on
her party dress, take the car to the local Grange hall, and dance. Shortly
before midnight, she'd be back at the mill gate to pick up Dad. During her
senior year, she bypassed Dad altogether and drove her own 1929 four-door
Chevrolet—which cost her folks $75—to the dances.

Bette wrote her class song in 1941, a sardonic parody of "Thanks for
the Memory," and shortly thereafter took her Chevy and the rest of her
belongings to Bremerton. Her brother-in-law, Herb Kraus, had found
her an office job there at the booming Naval Shipyard with Wright and
Hoffman, which eventually became the Howard S. Wright Construction

Company, builder of Seattle's Space Needle and several other major regional structures. As the only woman in the office—and a pretty one at that—she took a lot of grief. "The manager took one look at me and he said, 'Jesus Christ, Herb, what do we want with *that* in here?' That was my introduction to the world of crusty men."[1]

Bette Kennedy during her senior year of high school.
Snyder family photo

The job paid $33 a week, which seemed like a million to the wide-eyed Willapa teenager. Especially since she lived rent-free with her brother-in-law and her sister, Evelyn. She spent her money on gifts for her parents and, after World War II broke out, ferry rides across Puget Sound to Seattle to jitterbug the night away with the sailors on the hopping wooden floor of the Trianon Ballroom. Jazz musician Vic Meyers—who eventually became lieutenant governor and secretary of state—had a steady gig at the Trianon. Several national acts also performed there on a regular basis. Kennedy did not care much who was playing the music; she was just there to dance to it. At the end of the night, she slept on the return ferry, went to work the next day, and did it again that evening. "You didn't have to come home and sleep with anybody you danced with. We all just went our own ways," she said years later. "I'd just go back to my house and the sailors would go back wherever they were. It's a different world now."

Shortly after war's end in 1945, Kennedy and her friend, Lil, decided

Bette was a born charmer. That quality was still evident in 2009, when she and grandson Cole met Vice President Joe Biden. When Biden approached Bette, she told him, "Too bad you're not better looking." Biden cracked up and kissed her on the forehead.

they wanted to see what California had to offer, so Kennedy wrote a letter to the Los Angeles Chamber of Commerce asking what opportunities there were for women in the city. Someone wrote back and told her not to come. "They had enough young women in Hollywood," she said, "I guess they didn't need any more."

She and Lil went anyway, humming "California, Here I Come" as they hit the highway for the long drive south. Kennedy spent a few years in Southern California working various jobs, most notably as a receptionist at Hollywood Lincoln Mercury—Clark Gable was a client there—and as a secretary for Charles Goldring, business manager to such stars as Judy Garland, and, later, the blond bombshell, Jayne Mansfield. With an office on Sunset Boulevard in Beverly Hills, Goldring was one of a handful of people who represented a majority of the city's movie stars. He hired Kennedy because she had good handwriting and because he felt she looked like a movie star—perhaps à la Lauren Bacall. Sometimes stars danced in the small-town girl's own dazzling eyes, but mostly she dreamed of taking a year off work to travel the country—and shop all along the way. Bette Kennedy drove a red convertible and chronicled her fancy-free life with poetry:

> Bear witness to this, won't you, please
> Wherever you may be
> 'Cause I state right here and now
> A man'll never mean a thing to me.[2]

Five years after writing those male-bashing words, she met a man who meant everything to her. Six years after writing them, she married the Kelso Two-Stepper.

En route to their honeymoon in Portland, newlyweds Sid and Bette Snyder stopped to pose for a photo at Sid's mother's house in Longview. *Snyder family photo*

Extravagance was not in the cards. Sid and Bette's net worth was less than $100; A Justice-of-the-Peace wedding in a small room above a grocery store in downtown Long Beach was all they could afford. With friends Bob and Leona Sundstrom witnessing, the couple married on June 30, 1951, then drove an hour to the Pacific County Courthouse in South Bend to file the license. When they arrived, they were told they still needed witnesses. Bob and Leona were back the beach. So the sort-of newlyweds drove nearly another hour north to the Grays Harbor County Courthouse in Montesano, where they had friends who could sign for them. Then it was off to Portland for the honeymoon. Along the way, the couple stopped to visit Snyder's mother, who had remarried and moved from Kelso to Longview. A photo taken at that point was the first one of the newlyweds. They are standing beside Snyder's green, dented, and barely running four-door Plymouth. The car's chrome is polished to a shine, but still takes a backseat to the sparkling smiles of the happy couple.

Shortly after returning from the honeymoon, Sid left Long Beach on a monthlong fishing trip to Alaska. It was one of the many second jobs he took during the early years of his marriage. He also harvested oysters and cranberries, picked pine cones, worked at Costello's Market in Ilwaco, labored on road-construction projects, and set chokers for M.W. Logging Company. None of the jobs was particularly noteworthy, although his stint with M.W. Logging did command a brief mention in a history book written some 60 years after Snyder had laced his last pair of calk-soled boots. The company, the passage read, once "hired a husky lad from Long Beach named Sid Snyder, who, after a few months of setting chokers, realized that logging was not his calling."[3] Though he did not know it quite yet, Snyder had found his calling a year and a half before he had found his life partner.

That life-changing moment had taken place in January 1949, after the then-unemployed 22-year-old bumped into some friends from Long Beach who were talking about their jobs at the Capitol in Olympia. Snyder learned that the young men had acquired their jobs with the help of Long Beach's newly elected state representative, Ralph A. Smith.

Though young and moving down what appeared would be a blue-collar highway, Snyder was no political ignoramus. He had volunteered on a few local campaigns, regularly attended Democratic Party meetings, and, through those circles, had come to know Smith. Asking him for a low-level patronage job at the Capitol was by no means a stretch. Snyder gave Smith a call.

"Any chance of me getting a job in Olympia?"

"Why don't you come up Monday morning and I'll introduce you to the chief clerk."

Snyder jumped at the chance. The long, winding drive from the coast to the Capitol pushed to the limit a 1938 Buick he and some friends owned. One old friend said the car's hood fell off en route.

Republican Art Langlie was Washington's governor when Snyder arrived at the Capitol, and legislators were paid $100 a month. They met for 60 days every other year. The Legislative Building was essentially shuttered the rest of the time. Snyder was steeped in the who's who of local-level politics, but this was his first visit to Olympia. He arrived early, even after having to stop to retrieve his car's hood, then waited until late in the afternoon to meet with the chief clerk of the House, a Chesterfield-smoking institution named Silas Raymond "Si" Holcomb. The son of a state Supreme Court justice, Holcomb had arrived at the Capitol 32 years earlier for a part-time stenography job he need-ed to pay tuition at the University of Washington. Holcomb told Snyder the only job available was as an elevator operator—on the sleepy swing shift at $10 per week. Snyder took it. He got a room down the street at the five-story Hotel Olympian, then the state's political hub. While he was standing in the lobby waiting to check in, Snyder was hit by a sense of

Silas Raymond "Si" Holcomb and his ever-present Chesterfield cigarette.
Washington State Legislature

awe when a message came over the intercom:

"Senator Ray Hutchinson, please come to the front desk."

Snyder reported for duty the following day, and spent eight hours opening by hand the cage-like doors of the Legislative Building's four-passenger elevator. In time, Snyder became friendly with many of his powerful patrons, but never addressed them by their first name. It was always "Mister."

Snyder's best-known story from his short stint as House elevator operator comes from the day when a few misters, all Republicans, entered his elevator. As Snyder cranked the doors closed, one of the men asked what party he was affiliated with.

"Democrat, sir."

"Why Democrat?"

"My father was a Democrat, and my grandfather was a Democrat."

"If they had been horse thieves, son, would you have been a horse thief, too?"

"No, sir, I'd be a Republican."

Near the end of the session, Snyder saw an opportunity for advancement when a position in the bill room opened. Holcomb told Snyder the job was his, but his pay would remain the same.

The bill room was located directly off the Senate floor. Snyder's duties included sorting and filing copies of bills introduced in both the Senate and the House, and distributing copies of bills and amendments to the floors. "When they were debating we didn't have much to do," Snyder said. "We did our work when they were off the floor, most of it, even though people would come in the bill room and ask for copies of bills and amendments and so forth." It was during one of the down times that Snyder's hustle again helped him advance.

"One time Mister Holcomb came in and wanted some bills and everyone was kind of lounging around the tables that we worked from. I was sitting at one of those tables and Mister Holcomb walked in and wanted something, and I jumped right to it. So when the session was over he wanted to know if I wanted to stay and work after the session."

Snyder, third from left, became supervisor of the bill room in 1951. Among his charges was Bob Ford, far left, whose father, Robert M. Ford, was a longtime state representative from Kitsap County. *Washington State Legislature*

Assistant Chief Clerk Snyder takes a break in the bill room in 1957. *Snyder family photo*

Snyder stuck around for a month to help close down the legislative offices. Holcomb grew increasingly fond of Snyder's work ethic, and asked him to come back next session—in two years—to supervise the bill room. Snyder said he would, returned home, and landed a job at a service station south of Long Beach in Seaview. He was pumping gas there slightly before noon on April 13, 1949, when the largest-recorded earthquake in state history hit. Damage on the Long Beach Peninsula was negligible, but in Olympia, near the epicenter of the 7.1-magnitude quake, almost all large buildings were damaged to some extent, including all eight on the Capitol Campus. In the Legislative Building, broken windows and skylights shattered atop desks in the Senate and the House, and two dozen Cub Scouts were temporarily trapped inside the dome.

Snyder left the service station later that year, bounced from job to job—including those 30 post-honeymoon days on an Alaskan fishing boat—spent his spare time bowling, and helped Gordon Quornstrom, city editor of *The Longview Daily News*, campaign for a congressional seat.

Bowling was one of Snyder's favorite hobbies. Here he is in the early 1950s with his partners from the Sons of the Beaches team. *Snyder family photo*

Quornstrom lost to another newspaperman, Russell V. Mack of Hoquiam, the incumbent Republican.

In January 1951, Snyder returned to Olympia, boarded with a local family, and ran the bill room during a session that was followed by two budget-related special sessions—one in March and one in August. In early 1952, Snyder found a steady job stocking shelves at Chuck Conto's Sunset Grocery at the north end of Long Beach. The work came at the perfect time. His first child, Sidney Robert Snyder Jr., "Sidder" to family and friends, was born that Leap Day. The unique birthday was only part of Sid Jr.'s interesting arrival into the world. "There were five babies born that night at the tiny hospital in Ilwaco," Bette said. "I started having labor pains, but I didn't want to go to the hospital too soon so we went to the movies to see *Jim Thorpe: All American*. I had a chocolate milkshake, like a fool, and went up to the hospital." To free a bed for Bette, the hospital moved one of her migraine-suffering friends, Daisy Marsh, into the hall. When more expectant mothers began to arrive, including one carrying twins, Sid and another father climbed into the hospital's attic to retrieve extra beds.

The young Snyder family soon moved from a rented house in Seaview into a four-bedroom house on Idaho Street in Long Beach, two blocks east of the main drag lined with souvenir shops and clam-shovel rentals. They bought the house for $5,600—$400 of that for the furniture—thanks to a $2,500 loan from Bette's parents, who recently had received a small inheritance.

Snyder returned to work at the Capitol prior to the 1953 session, but stuck around only a short while, mostly to help Holcomb clean out his desk. Republicans had gained control of the House the previous fall. As was customary, they had chosen their own man to serve as chief clerk. Snyder's life outside Olympia that year more than made up for any excitement he may have missed inside it.

He was 18 months into his job at Sunset Grocery when a friendly gesture changed his life. In July 1953, a Sunset regular named C.J. "Bud" Underwood told Snyder about a small store in Seaview he had heard was on the market. The store's owner, Bob Larson, had suffered a heart attack over Fourth of July weekend and his doctor had advised him not to return to work, Underwood related.

"Why don't you see what he wants for it."

"I don't have any money."

"Maybe I can help you."

Snyder learned that Larson wanted $12,200, a princely sum considering roughly half that cost was for some basic shelving, a meat case, and an uncooled produce rack. Underwood, a supervisor with the Deep River Timber Company, loaned Snyder $13,200 at a whopping 12 percent interest. That included $1,000 in cash for the till. On August 7, Snyder took over Seaview Market, paying $40 a month in rent. The building wasn't part of the deal. By the end of the month, he had done $7,600 worth of business, easily surpassing Larson's usual gross.

Seaview Market eventually became Sid's Market, a one-man operation. Snyder would cut and wrap customers' meat, then move around the L-shaped counter to ring up their purchase. There were three shopping carts, but the aisles of the 1,200-square-foot building were so narrow that it was difficult to wheel them through it. A fire did substantial damage shortly after Snyder took over. He did the repairs himself.

His second child, Karen, was born a little more than a month after he had become a store owner, on September 24, 1953. For the next few years, Snyder focused on building his business. Although Democrats regained control of the House and Holcomb was brought back as their assistant chief clerk, Snyder did not return to Olympia for the 1955 session. He had too much going on at Long Beach to break free. His third and final child, Sally, was

Sid butchers meat while Bette arranges items in the Snyders' first store in the 1950s. The store's aisles were so narrow that it was difficult to wheel shopping carts through them. *Snyder family photo*

The proud father stands with babes in arms—Karen in his right one
and Sally in his left. *Snyder family photo*

born that December 9. Bette, who had worked many hours at the store,
now stayed home. Dad worked seven days a week, intent on never drop-
ping below the $100-a-day goal he had set for himself.

The Long Beach Peninsula was highlighted on Snyder's life map. Olympia
was hardly a dot, let alone a capital-symbolizing star, off in the upper-right
corner.

Snyder became Chief Clerk Si Holcomb's assistant in 1957. *Washington State Legislature*

Four ▪ Olympia Fever

R AY MOORE THOUGHT SI HOLCOMB was a damn good chief clerk but not much of a teacher.

Although Holcomb enjoyed bipartisan respect, his year-end instructor-evaluation form from Moore—had such a thing existed in the 1940s—would have been filled with boxes check-marked "unsatisfactory" and "needs improvement." Moore, a Seattle stock broker, had been tabbed by majority Republicans to serve as Holcomb's assistant for the 1947 session. The GOP plan had been to keep the veteran Democrat in place so Moore could learn all there was to know about the office, then replace him for the next session. But Holcomb shrewdly was having none of it. He wanted to keep the job he had held for 14 years, and was not willing to help the political newbie in the least. "Holcomb never let me learn anything," Moore groused. "He gave me a clipboard every morning: 'Today I want you to check and see if all the cuspidors are here.' The next day the hat racks; the next day the chairs; the next day the filing cabinets. Although I sat on the rostrum with him, I never knew anything about the job when the session adjourned."[1] It wouldn't have mattered much in the long run. Harry S. Truman's re-election in 1948 helped Democrats gain 39 seats and a 67-32 majority in Washington's House. There was no way the well-liked Holcomb would have been replaced by Moore—or anyone, for that matter. Moore later switched parties and served 16 years as a state senator. His institutional memory and flinty observations became legendary.

Sid Snyder held a much different opinion of Holcomb's teaching abilities. To him, the older man was a mentor—a man who had given him the opportunity of a lifetime; promoted him when he showed hustle; a man who had not forgotten him during the years when circumstance had required him to forgo Olympia to mind the store. So when Holcomb called Snyder one day in December 1956, Snyder listened intently as Holcomb spoke:

"I'd like you to come up and be my assistant chief clerk."

Snyder was in no position to leave Long Beach. He practically lived at his store, and ate only when Bette drove down the road to deliver him a meal. However, it did not take long for him to give Holcomb an answer:

"Sure. I'll come."

Snyder's decision to return to Olympia seemed illogical, but only to those who did not know him. Work always had been something he prided himself on, and there was something about the political process that always drew him in. Bette called it "the fever for Olympia," and when Holcomb threw another virus his way, Snyder's temperature shot up. "[Working in Olympia], to me, is the ultimate," Snyder said. "It's part of a process you can't be part of anywhere else—unless you move to another state."

Before Snyder could head out of town, he had business to take care of. He hired someone to cut meat at the market each evening, and, via a newspaper ad in *The Oregonian*, the family hired a high school girl from Portland to live at their house and help care for the children. That freed Bette to take over the checkstand, stock shelves, and help with the book-keeping. It was not your typical family arrangement, but it worked for the Snyders.

In January, Snyder returned to a Capitol that had changed in many ways since he had last worked there. Thanks in no small part to a right-to-work initiative that had drawn blue-collar voters to the polls, Democrats now had firm control of the Legislature and Albert D. Rosellini, a charismatic Italian-American lawyer from Tacoma, was governor. Former University of Washington football player and head coach John Cherberg had ridden the same tide to what would be a long tenure as lieutenant governor, and rising-star Republicans Dan Evans and Charles P. Moriarty Jr. bucked the trend to win their first terms in the House.

Snyder's assignment was not easy. He was stepping into the shoes of Ward Bowden—a weekly newspaper owner who had been promoted to secretary of the Senate. The new Senate majority leader, R.R. "Bob" Greive, believed Bowden "was the most knowledgeable man in state government on the Legislature and legislative procedures."[2] Snyder was not averse to learning. He studied parliamentary procedure under Holcomb, a master, and later taught classes on the process to freshman legislators. He helped revise Holcomb's lengthy handbook of legislative names, dates, and maps. He crossed the marbled hall to ask questions of Bowden. The two became good friends.

Ward Bowden was assistant chief clerk of the House prior to Snyder. Bowden left the job to become secretary of the Senate. Snyder eventually would succeed Bowden in that post as well. *Washington State Legislature*

One of Snyder's main duties as assistant chief clerk was to assign bills to committees. Sometimes the choice was obvious, but other times, especially when members would debate and vote on the particular committee where they felt the bill should go, it was a difficult task. At the end of each day and oftentimes during session breaks, Snyder would pore over bills to try to determine which direction they should head. He consulted with Holcomb on difficult decisions. Once the decision was made, the bills moved to the speaker. At the time and for years to come, that was the wily John L. O'Brien, who had created so many committees that every non-freshman member either was a committee chair or a member of the Rules Committee.

"[The process of choosing a committee] was lengthy because it had the title on the bill and the titles oftentimes referred to a whole lot of RCWs," Snyder said, referring to the Revised Code of Washington. Bills were time-stamped by Snyder so he could not be blamed for holding them up. Snyder also would help draft amendments if members asked. He earned $32 a day, and they were long days down the stretch of a session.

Snyder's learning curve became much steeper near the end of the session, due to a different kind of curve that had been unintentionally thrown by his boss. With 10 days left in a session that Rosellini was determined to see end in 60 days—no matter how long the clocks had to be ignored—Holcomb vanished. One of Si's problems was alcohol. Snyder was forced to take over his mentor's duties. "Si would get on these binges," Snyder said. "I went down to his hotel room one time when he hadn't been to work. He'd get up and go into the bathroom quite often. Well, I wasn't bright enough to know at the time he had a bottle in there. So he'd go in and he was getting drunker as time went on. And then they took him away and sent him to a clinic in Portland to dry him out."

Snyder had never been through the crucible of a conference committee to reconcile legislation. In fact, he hardly knew what a conference committee was. "There were so many things going on that I had never experienced. These guys are giants and I was just a lowly flunky compared to Si and others." Snyder leaned heavily on Bowden for advice, and visited him frequently. After every question Snyder asked, the former assistant chief clerk would shoot back with, "What do *you* think you do?" Snyder would give his best answer. Then Bowden would correct him if he was wrong. Holcomb's rookie stand-in had been able to muddle through in his absence—thanks to several long nights and days and timely advice from an old hand.

Holcomb reappeared for part of a day five days before the end of the session, then left and was not seen again at the Capitol until 30 days after the session had ended. Many legislators held a grudge against the longtime clerk for this and other reasons. Speaker O'Brien was one of them: "[He] wasn't even around for closing ceremonies. He was holed up in a motel room someplace. I proceeded to take him off the payroll. The staff didn't think he should be paid and I just took him off. I didn't have much choice, but he never forgot that."[3]

A 34-year-old Snyder hard at work as Si Holcomb's assistant in 1961. *Washington State Legislature*

Holcomb's disappearing act was just one of many points of contention between him and O'Brien, who served as speaker from 1955-1963. "He and John O'Brien didn't get along well because one of the things Si did, which I didn't know for a long time, was he sold services to lobbyists," Snyder said. "In other words, he had a system where lobbyists would get bills delivered to their hotel rooms or motel rooms and he would get a fee for that."

Never a heavy drinker, Snyder even abstained from social drinking when it got near the end of a session. He feared others saying, "If that Sid Snyder hadn't have been half drunk he wouldn't have screwed up on that bill." When Snyder did imbibe, it would be a glass or two of wine, a beer or a couple cocktails during a social function. When left to concoct a drink on his own, simplicity was key. In *Gordon Walgren's Majority Leader's Cookbook*, "Sid's Tonic" is the shortest recipe in all 252 pages. "After a long day, or even a short day," Snyder suggested: "To one chilled cocktail glass add: 1 ample jigger of Beefeaters Gin over lots of ice and toss in a fresh piece of lime."[4] Some legislators—such as Representative Damon Canfield of Yakima—did not drink at all. Others drank often, succumbing to the times—and the fact that they were away from home—taking no time to burn through the free case of beer delivered each Monday from various state breweries. With group dinners nearly every night, there were plenty of opportunities to drink. Even at the Capitol itself.

Senator William Gissberg, an outspoken Democrat from Everett, said when he was first elected in 1953, it "seemed like any senator that drank would be able to keep a bottle in his filing cabinet drawer."[5] For two decades, there even was a semi-formal spot in the Legislative Building for members to toss back a few. The improvised bar had been the creation of Ralph C. "Brig" Young, a Cle Elum barber and Pittsburgh native first elected to the House in 1941. Early in his legislative career, Young had installed his barber's chair in a fourth-floor storage room and began giving free haircuts. Oftentimes the waiting line would spill out of the small room and into the hallway. Young soon added a discarded davenport, and then a refrigerator filled with beer, wine, and liquor. The smoke-filled, windowless room quickly became the place to hang out. But when there was no line, members had a hard time figuring out exactly which of the many nondescript storage rooms was the ex-officio bar. Young solved that by crisscrossing two pieces of white tape to make an "X" on his room's door. Thus, it became Committee Room X, and the site of some implausible stories. Elmer "Bud" Huntley, a Republican legislator from Whitman County, recalled one of them: Young was in the middle of giving a haircut and left the room for a moment to take a call. While he was away, Huntley said, "This one fellow reached into the refrigerator and got some Scotch and poured a tumbler of Scotch. He looked around for water and didn't find any, but he found the barber bench." He mixed the booze with the clear contents of a glass he found on the bench, and handed the drink to another man. "He took a swig of it and his eyes lit up like a pinball machine. It was formaldehyde. He used to dip his combs in it." A doctor was called and the drinker sent to the bathroom to vomit. Happily, "he recovered nicely."[6]

Committee Room X continued in various forms even after Young left the Legislature in 1957. The Senate soon created its own version of Committee Room X, sans barber, across the rotunda. Both rooms lasted until 1963, when Representative Don Miles of Olympia said he was going to introduce a bill to ban alcohol in the Legislative Building and do away with the committee rooms. In its January 17, 1963, issue *The Arlington Times* reported on "the horrified discovery made by Don Miles, Olympia attorney and local and regional church leader, that there have been two committee rooms, labeled committee Room 'X' just outside the House and Senate where a jaded and frustrated solon could go for a refresher in case of an emergency."[7] The article also contained anecdotal evidence implying that Si Holcomb was not the only problem drinker on the premises: The Olympia liquor store took in some $42,000 more in 1961 when the Legislature was in session than it did in 1962 when it was not. Miles' bill never passed, but the negative publicity he generated spelled an end to the two rooms. Some maintain Olympia has never been the same.

A dried-out Holcomb returned to work prior to the start of the 1959 session, and Snyder returned as his right-hand man. House Democrats now outnumbered Republicans by a two-to-one margin. O'Brien was re-elected speaker. Snyder's good friend, Julia Butler Hansen of Cathlamet, who four years earlier had nearly become the state's first female speaker, was elected speaker pro-tem. The House majority leader was August "Augie" Mardesich, a former commercial fisherman first appointed to the House in 1950 under tragic circumstances. Mardesich's father and his brother, a first-term state representative, had been killed in 1949 when their family's 65-foot fishing boat capsized off the coast of Alaska. Augie survived the wreck by clinging to a piece of debris until he was rescued by another boat. He was appointed to fill his brother's vacant seat. He became a master of the dance of legislation.

Some top-notch, moderate Republicans also had been elected to the House the previous November. Among them were a cerebral Ivy League lawyer, Slade Gorton, and Seattle businessman Joel Pritchard, one of the architects of the rise of post-war, progressive Republican politics in Washington state. Together with second-termers Evans and Moriarty, they shared a rented home on South Columbia Street in Olympia. "[The four men] and a lot of others were referred to as 'Dan Evans Republicans,'" Snyder said. "There was a big advantage to them [living together]. Naturally, you're talking politics most of the time and about what's going on in the political world."

Possessing the governorship and majorities in both chambers, the Democrats figured to have an easy go of lawmaking in 1959, even with the smart young Republicans resisting at every turn. That was not the case. The Democrats suffered through several intraparty squabbles, many over the budget and which tax was going to be levied, or created, to balance it. In the end, and despite a threat from Greive to step down as Senate majority leader because of it, an increase in the state sales tax won out.

Sid's Market was doing $200,000 a year in business by 1960, but with room to expand in short supply, that likely was the most it would ever make. To grow, Snyder borrowed $11,500—again from Bud Underwood and again at 12 percent interest—to purchase an entire block one street north of the current market, on Pacific Avenue in Seaview between 44th and 45th streets. There were six cottages on the new property, and Snyder had them moved. His mother eventually moved into one. Next, he built a 5,200-square-foot market in the middle of the 40,000-square-foot parcel. He thought: "Oh, my God, that's all I'll ever need."

When Julia Butler Hansen announced her candidacy for Congress in April 1960, Snyder stepped in to lead her campaign in Pacific County. Hansen was simultaneously running to fill the remainder of Congressman Russell Mack's term—he had died on the House floor in March—and also for a spot in the 87th Congress. Hansen won both, thanks in part, Snyder feels, to the sensitivity she exhibited for Mack's mourners prior to entering the race. "You know, your phone rings, 'Sid, Russell Mack just died. Are you going to be running [for his seat]?' 'Well, I probably will.' That was the answer from most people. Julia's answer was, 'I'm going to wait until the gentleman's funeral before I announce the decision.' That looked pretty good next to people that were saying 'I'm going to run.' "

Hansen had moved to Washington, D.C., when Snyder returned to Olympia in January 1961 to again serve as assistant chief clerk. Holcomb was back as his boss, but exactly which speaker both men would be working for took a while to be determined. O'Brien was seeking his fourth term and had to fight and bargain his way to re-election through an initially split caucus.

Snyder was now in his fourth session as assistant chief clerk. That experience and his sunny personality had earned him some political power. He used some of both behind the scenes to help get the Astoria-Megler Bridge built across the Columbia River in his neck of the woods. The bridge long had been a pet project of silver-haired state Senator Bob Bailey, a gentlemanly South Bend Democrat. In 1957, Bailey began discussing a partnership with the State of Oregon for the ambitious project. He felt such a span would be a win-win for both states. His legislative district would benefit from additional tourists and other shoppers continuing north. As things stood, a ferry was the only way to cross the Columbia there, and it was a long way around. The shorter crossing would also open up some jobs to people in his district. Oregon would benefit by subtraction: Its ferry was losing roughly a quarter-million dollars each year, and runs could be delayed or scrapped altogether when waters were choppy—often the case in the winter.

In 1961, Bailey's bill cruised through the Senate. Yet the House did not show much interest. Near the end of the session, Snyder mentioned the bill to Brig Young, who said he would pull it for a vote. Bailey's bridge bill was one of the last passed by the House that year, and Rosellini happily signed it into law. Construction on the $24 million, 4.1-mile span—the longest continuous-truss bridge in North America—began the following year, and the "Bridge to Nowhere," as many Oregon residents called it, opened in the summer of 1966. On July 29, Snyder, with 14-year-old Sid Jr. beside him, was fifth in line to drive across from the Washington side. When father—dressed in suit and tie—and son hit Astoria, they immediately turned around and came back, making them the first round-trippers. It was an early birthday present for Snyder. He turned 40 the following day.

Near the end of 1961, tragedy nearly struck the Snyder family when Bette, the kids, and several other families were enjoying a Sunday afternoon swim at a public pool in Long Beach. While Sid Jr. and 5-year-old Sally were splashing away near one end of the pool, 8-year-old Karen was practicing a face-down floating technique and ended up drifting into the deep end. Bette, who was in the pool, was horrified when she noticed her daughter missing. Minutes later Karen was found, still face down but now unconscious, under the diving board. Her stomach distended from the water she had swallowed, the child was given mouth-to-mouth resuscitation by a volunteer firefighter named Wayne O'Neil, who

Sid, with son Sid Jr. in the passenger seat, was the first person to make a round-trip drive across the newly opened Astoria-Megler Bridge in July 1966. *Snyder family photo*

Snyder takes the oath of office in 1967. *Washington State Legislature*

worked for *The Chinook Observer*. O'Neil was at the pool that day with his own family and had just viewed a film on resuscitation techniques. "It required 10 or more resuscitation efforts to again start the little girl's breathing," read an article that week in O'Neil's paper. "She had turned blue, and had no signs of life."[8] Sid's Market was closed at the time of the accident, but Sid was at the store cutting deer meat for customers. He arrived at the pool at the same time as the ambulance. The family followed the emergency vehicle down the highway to Ocean Beach Hospital in Ilwaco. Nearly two gallons of water were pumped from Karen's stomach, and she stayed in the hospital overnight. Her first question when she came to: "Will I be going to swimming lessons tomorrow?" She had been afraid she would be punished for nearly dying and would not be allowed to revisit the pool.

One column to the left of the paper's story on the close call was a small

Sid's Market in Seaview, photographed from across Pacific Avenue, in 1960.
Snyder family photo

article headlined "Local Deer Kill Took Swing Upward." In it, Sid Snyder's name is listed along with 28 others who had reported having tagged a deer that week. Many of them had taken their kill to Sid's Market for processing.

Five ▪ "A Portly Grocer"

O N REALITY TELEVISION, they call it a "pact." The contestants secretly meet—at least as secretly as possible when video cameras are recording every move—and combine forces to send someone home from Borneo, Panama, or Palau. They cast the week's top threat off the island, advance themselves and the group, and retire to their fireside sleeping bags for a bite of butok and a side of boiled balut without any real-world ramifications.

In 1963, four decades before such shenanigans commandeered America's airwaves, Sid Snyder had a front-row seat to the session-long consequences of a pact that not only occurred in real life but also changed the political culture of his state for years to come.

The accord, which legislative historian Don Brazier said led to "argu-ably the single most dramatic series of events in the history of the State and the Territory,"[1] was sealed the day before the start of the 1963 session in a meeting at a rented house at the end of a "long dirt road flanked by towering old-growth evergreens"[2] in West Olympia. Snyder, the assistant chief clerk, was there, his ticket handed to him by his boss an hour prior to the gathering while he was out on the rostrum stenciling documents and feeding them into a mimeograph. "Get in the car," Si Holcomb told him. "We are heading to Cooper Point to review a script for the next day."

Snyder drove because Holcomb's eyesight was fading. He was stunned as he pulled into the driveway: "My God. There's Tom Copeland's car." Snyder knew there was no reason for Copeland, a Walla Walla Republican and the previous session's whip, to be at a routine script-review session. Snyder's suspicion grew stronger as he entered the house. Five more

Assistant Chief Clerk Snyder's official House portrait. *Washington State Legislature*

Republicans—Don Eldridge, Dan Evans, Elmer Johnston, Joel Pritchard, and Slade Gorton—were there, as were Democrats Bill Day, Dick Kink, Chet King, Margaret Hurley, Bill McCormick, and Bob Perry.*

The attending Democrats were dissidents willing to join forces with minority Republicans in a bargain to get their guy, which happened to be "Big Daddy" Day, elected speaker over John O'Brien. As Day later said, he and his cohorts were upset with their party's platform; they wanted to "hold the line on taxes," didn't like the fact that their majority had dwindled during O'Brien's four terms as speaker, and felt the state should develop a "liberal program not based on government ownership."[4]

Realizing he likely was brought along only as Holcomb's chauffeur, Snyder sat slack-jawed and quiet through the evening as the two-party coalition planned its coup. "Everything was all set that night," Snyder said. "Of course I couldn't go back and say anything, because we worked for all of the members." Snyder did admit to confiding in two people: Holcomb's

---

* Some accounts say Pritchard was not present—even Pritchard's own recollection. But Snyder swore he was, and, years later, Gorton told an interviewer that while admitting his memory may be playing tricks on him, "I assume that he was [there] because he was in everything else."

Snyder and Si Holcomb stand during a meeting of the House Rules Committee in 1965.
Snyder's right hand is resting on the shoulder of P.J. Gallagher, and Joel Pritchard
is in front of Holcomb. To the right of Pritchard heading clockwise are Don Eldridge,
Jim Andersen, Bob Goldsworthy, Tom Copeland, Avery Garrett, Bob Schaefer,
Frank Brouillet, John O'Brien, Bill "Big Daddy" Day, Ray Olsen, Eric Braun,
Paul Conner, Bill May, and Dick Taylor. *Bob Miller, Washington State Legislature*

secretary, Lucille Rohrbeck, and his friend, Senator Bob Bailey, whom
Snyder rated as "the most highly respected legislator in his time."[5] He did
not tell O'Brien, although he did go into his office to wish him luck.

The six Republicans caucused the next morning to inform their colleagues of the plan, solicit input, and tweak the scheme before heading to
the floor at noon for the vote on speaker. Three candidates were nominated: O'Brien, Day and Evans. O'Brien received 45 votes, Day six; Evans
took all 48 Republican votes. On the second roll call, Evans again received
all 48 Republican votes, O'Brien got 44 and Day seven. On the third roll
call, the coalition sprang the trap. The Republicans—with the exception
of one who stayed with Evans—all voted for Day, as did 10 Democrats,
giving him 57 votes to O'Brien's 41. The coup was a success. Day, the dis-
sident Democrat from Spokane, was elected speaker of the House. O'Brien

was livid. He called the dissidents "dishonest and immoral," and said the Republicans were guilty of a "low type of political maneuvering."[6]

Snyder saw it all go down from his front-row seat next to Holcomb on the rostrum. "It was pretty heated. I know O'Brien was devastated. The galleries were packed, and the aisles of the chambers were packed. There were lots of people watching." Snyder met with Speaker Day the following morning in an upstairs committee room to brief him on procedural matters. "He was completely in the dark on what he would need to do."

Snyder eventually confessed to O'Brien that he had been at the West Olympia house the night before, and O'Brien said he understood why Snyder had not said anything. The rest of the 60-day session was emotional and divisive, as might be expected from a House so abnormally divided. "I just went on doing my job like I thought I should be doing, and if people asked me for advice I would give it to them," Snyder said. "If they took it, fine. If they asked me questions, I'd try to answer them and be as fair as I could. If somebody asked me something, I wouldn't run and tell somebody else that somebody else was going to make a motion to do this. You work for all the members, and you don't pass on little secrets."

Later that year, Snyder ended up riding in the same car as Governor Rosellini on the way back from an event on the Long Beach Peninsula. The governor asked him if he would consider running against coalition member Chet King of Raymond in 1964. Snyder was flattered but uninterested. "I just didn't think I was prepared, if I could get elected, to spend the time that was necessary." The governor was not the only person to try to recruit Snyder for King's seat in the House. Bob Bailey did, too, even going as far as filling out some of the initial paperwork for Snyder.

The Lyndon Johnson-led tide that swept the country on Election Day 1964, worked its way west from D.C. to Olympia. Democrats maintained control of the Legislature, although the state's voters held true to their independent nature and replaced Rosellini with the youngest governor in state history, 39-year-old Dan Evans.

The 1965 Legislature, still dealing with coalition-related bitterness, faced a difficult initial task. A federal court order had declared that no new legislation, save for a bill to address ongoing expenses, could be acted upon until a redistricting bill was passed. This was desperate stuff. The majority party was in the catbird seat to draw favorable new district boundaries. Because Evans would not be sworn in until the session's third day, the Democrats set out to pass their plan during the first two days so it could be signed into law by Rosellini. Otherwise, it would face a certain veto by Evans. Frantically searching for votes, the Democrats in both chambers were unable to come up with a bill both could agree upon. Had they, the Republicans had a contingency plan. They were poised to speed up Evans' swearing in, even securing a Supreme Court Justice to administer the oath as soon as the clock struck midnight Wednesday.

Snyder's memories of those dramatic three days include a rarely told, what-might-have-been tale. On the session's second day, Si Holcomb had slyly kept the House speaker and the Senate president from signing election certificates, as was custom. Had the Republicans sworn in Evans just after midnight, Holcomb knew the new governor technically would not have been in office—absent a signed certificate of election. "So, hypothetically now," Snyder said, "what would have happened if Rosellini had signed the bill at 10 o'clock on the third day and Dan Evans had been sworn in 9½ hours earlier than that? Was he officially certified? That would have made a hell of a court case, but it never came to fruition." Snyder told Evans the story years later, and they both laughed.

So contentious was the redistricting bill—with dueling teams of number-crunchers working late every night, Slade Gorton vs. Bob Greive—that Evans ended up vetoing a couple of plans the Legislature passed. He finally signed one into law on the 47th day of the 60-day session. Redistricting left a backlog of bills. During the first 47 days, bills had been introduced, referred in and out of committees, and amended on the floor. But none could be voted on, as per the court order. Then, logjam broken, more than 225 bills were passed into law during the last 13 days. Countless others were passed during the 54-day extra session that immediately followed. The 1965

Legislature finally adjourned on May 7.

Shortly before the regular session ended, at 8:29 a.m. on April 29, another huge earthquake struck the Puget Sound region—the second of Snyder's tenure at the Capitol. This one registered 6.7 on the Richter scale. Snyder was at the Tyee Motor Inn, a popular Tumwater motel and bar where much of the state's real business was done after hours. He was about to leave his room. When he finally got to the Capitol, broken glass and rubble was everywhere, including the House floor. A shard of glass was stuck, spear-like, into the back of a chair, right where a member's head might have been had the quake hit an hour or so later.

Snyder and Holcomb worked the unusual '65 session under the new speaker, Bob Schaefer, who had replaced one-termer Big Daddy Day. Schaefer was a young, well-liked lawyer from Vancouver. Snyder felt Schaefer had the perfect temperament to deal with a post-coalition House. "He was a person who I think of as a healer. He looked at politics and legislation as the art of compromise. You give a little and you take a little and then you come up with a solution." Schaefer was the latest in an interesting succession of speakers Snyder would work under during his 20 years as a House employee.

On Thanksgiving Day 1965, Si Holcomb—"Mister Holcomb" to his protégé—died of cancer at age 70. Shortly before Holcomb's death, the Snyders had visited him in a Bellevue hospital where he lay ravaged. "We went directly to his room. I looked in and went back out and said, 'I got the wrong room.' But I hadn't."

Snyder immediately assumed the 30-year veteran's duties and served as chief clerk until 1967. Though administrative moves in the Legislature rarely made the news cycle, this one did, thanks to Associated Press correspondent Leroy Hittle. The lead to Hittle's story, given the circumstances of Snyder's promotion, was a little light: "A portly grocer as jolly as Santa has quickly moved in to take over the duties of chief clerk of the state House of Representatives."[8] The story ran in newspapers across the state, including the December 20, 1965, issue of the *Walla Walla Union-Bulletin*, which

Snyder may have been away from home a lot but his family often came to visit him in Olympia, too. From left here are Sally, Karen, Sid, Bette, and Sid Jr. *Snyder family photo*

placed it under a large headline, "Jolly and Portly Grocer New House Chief Clerk." It was all true. He was a grocer, invariably good-humored and, in those days, round-faced and big-waisted—240 pounds at his heaviest. He didn't mind being "portly." It was a badge of honor. "Nobody likes a skinny grocer," he often said.

The article also made note of several of the organizations with which Snyder had been involved. He was director of the Washington State Food Dealers Association, and past president of the Long Beach Lions Club and the Ilwaco Chamber of Commerce. It also mentioned Snyder's family, which was chipping in at Sid's Market. Sid Jr., now 13 years old, had been able to make change and parse shipping cases for a decade, and had done so wearing aprons made by his grandmother. Twelve-year-old Karen and Sally, who was 10, had their specialties, too, stocking shelves and helping with inventory. In high school, the two girls mostly worked summers: Sally in health and beauty aids and Karen in the meat department. There was no mention in the article of the good deeds Snyder did that went unnoticed by most. Such as the time a local man ordered a side of beef from Sid's Market and, before he came back to pay for it, died of a heart attack. Snyder picked up the tab, but told the man's widow her husband had paid it.

In 1967 and 1969, even though the Republicans had captured the majority, Snyder was brought back as assistant to their new chief clerk. That was the handiwork of the new speaker, gentlemanly Don Eldridge of Mount Vernon, and the new majority leader, Slade Gorton. It was unheard of for a member of the minority party to serve in either of the top clerk positions, but everyone respected Snyder. He kept his word—and secrets—and by now was a master parliamentarian. Gorton stipulated that henceforth the assistant clerk's job would always go to someone from the minority party. Part of that was to protect his party's interests; the other part was to protect Sid. Eldridge even offered Snyder the same pay as the chief clerk. Snyder turned the raise down, but took the job.

Eldridge believed Snyder "added a great deal to the operation because of his tremendous knowledge and the fact that he got along well with everybody. Sid took care of a lot of the mechanical things and it worked out very well."[7] Snyder, moreover, got along well with the new chief clerk, Malcolm "Dutch" McBeath of Bellingham, Eldridge's former roommate and an ex-House member. Though McBeath technically was head of the operation, Snyder was the one Eldridge turned to when he needed help on the rostrum, particularly when parliamentary procedure was in question. "I'd swirl around in my chair, or get up and advise him on it," Snyder said. That Snyder was running the show—his pay was now $65 a day—was obvious to other members as well. Snyder said that was not due to any shortcomings on McBeath's part. It was simply a matter of him having more experience.

When Snyder was away in Olympia, it was business as usual at the market and the big house the Snyders recently had purchased just off the beach on Boulevard Avenue. The kids missed their dad but received special benefits, such as the opportunity to work as legislative pages from an early age. In later years, while Dad was working, the Snyder ladies traveled the world to attend figure skating world championships and two Olympic Games. Each year, when the Long Beach Peninsula hosted "the world's longest garage sale," 28 miles of household flotsam, the Snyders hosted the biggest and most popular one. It was one of two major projects Bette undertook each year—Christmas being the other. She would spend six months working on each. Most years, hundreds of people would be lined up outside the Snyder home on the first Saturday morning in August, waiting for the gong to be struck to get their hands on the best stuff—brand-name clothing the kids had outgrown, art, and other goods previously owned by the Snyders, Cherbergs, other politicians and 30 or so families and friends. "People would just hit that place like you wouldn't believe," former Senate Majority Leader Gordon Walgren said. The Walgrens never missed participating in the big sale. "Somebody would have to be in charge of security—we had things spread out all over the yard. We had to watch people coming in from the perimeters." Dinner at the famous Ark Restaurant was, of course, on Sid and Bette—and Sunday brunch at their home was, too. "It was the social event of the year for a lot of us," Walgren said.

Things were happy at home in close-knit Long Beach. That was a good thing, because everyone knew that—had they wanted to—it would have been difficult to get Snyder to surrender his part-time passion at the Capitol.

The Snyders' annual garage sale was a must-attend for those on the Long Beach Peninsula—and beyond. Crowds lined up at the foot of the driveway waiting for the sale to open. *Snyder family photo*

House Speaker Don Eldridge poses for a photo with Snyder and his daughter Karen, who was serving as a page. *Snyder family photo*

Sally Snyder also paged as a child. She is seen here with her dad in 1971. *Snyder family photo*

Snyder, far right, and Si Holcomb, to Snyder's right wearing glasses, worked the 1965 session under Speaker Bob Schaefer, seen here standing at the back of the rostrum. *Washington State Legislature*

Six ▪ Changing Chambers

Neil Armstrong took one giant step for mankind. The war in Vietnam reached its terrible peak, and the protests at home did, too. Half a million people gathered on a farm in upstate New York to party in the name of peace. And in Olympia, women's groups marched outside the Capitol for an entire session, demanding legalized abortion. February saw a band of armed Black Panthers from Seattle join the tumult to complain about racism. Four of the Panthers were invited into the Senate's powerful Ways and Means Committee by its chairman, Martin Durkan, to air their grievances. One told the committee, "You can ask all the questions you want, but I'm going to tell *you*. You can sit and listen. We're going to take our time because we know we won't be wanted back."[1]

Nineteen-sixty-nine was one of history's most unforgettable years. But legislatively, at least in the state of Washington, it was a dud. That year's 120-day session—60 regular, 60 special—was the longest since 1909. Outside, people were protesting everything. Inside, House Democrats staged a temporary walkout over a Republican-called, all-night budget session. But little significant legislation was moved. "Many observers could not remember a less productive session," Don Brazier wrote in one of his histories, adding that 1969 was "a disappointment."[2] Brazier's assessment is backed up by the fact that Sid Snyder—whom *The Seattle Times* once said has an "unfailing memory" that yields a "never-ending source of stories of the old days"—had little legislative-related tales to tell from the year.[3] But that does not mean the year was story-less. Far from it. The events of 1969 were among the most impactful of Snyder's life.

At the Capitol, near the end of the session, something happened that benefitted him in the long run, but he certainly did not welcome it at the time. On the morning of May 2, Snyder had gone to visit Ward Bowden, the secretary of the Senate and his longtime friend and adviser. But Bowden was not in his office. He had called his secretary, Florence Kenderesi, to say he had "the crud" and would be in about noon. Soon after Snyder returned to the House, Gene Prince, the sergeant at arms, "came running in from the back of the chamber and said, 'Did you know Ward Bowden died?' Apparently, he was having a heart attack and didn't know it."

Snyder's Capitol career path had mimicked that of the slightly older Bowden. Both had worked in the bill room. Both had become its supervisor. Both had been assistant chief clerks in the House, and were well-liked by legislators on both sides of the aisle. Senators Bob Bailey, Bill Gissberg, and Augie Mardesich almost immediately began campaigning for Snyder to succeed Bowden. Snyder told them he was interested, but he had two points to make. First, he wanted to make it clear that, with his store flourishing and ready to expand, he would not be able to spend as much time in Olympia as Bowden had. Second, he wondered about the status of Bowden's assistant, Don Wilson, who also wanted the job and was the favored candidate of Majority Leader Bob Greive.

At dinnertime on May 12, the marathon session's final day, Speaker Eldridge sent Snyder to the Senate to deliver a message to Bailey. When Snyder arrived, the Democrats were caucusing, so Sid sat on the couch and waited. He struck up a conversation with the caucus clerk, Mike Gallagher, who told him an important vote was taking place. Shortly, Wes Uhlman, a future Seattle mayor, emerged from the meeting and approached Snyder. "Congratulations, you're the new secretary of the Senate." It was all but a done deal. Around midnight, Snyder walked on the Senate floor to deliver an armload of bills from the House just in time to see someone on the floor throwing a profane fit. Wilson then stormed off the rostrum. The official vote had just taken place, and Snyder had formally beaten Wilson for the job.

With the Senate workroom staff in tears over their guy's loss, Snyder immediately took his spot on the Senate rostrum. "I walked in as assistant chief clerk of the House of Representatives, and I stayed. I never went back." Wilson soon moved over to the House to replace Snyder.

The Senate job was considered a promotion, although as assistant chief clerk Snyder had performed many of the same duties. In fact, the chief clerk of the House and the secretary of the Senate essentially had the same job. The title—secretary—was a misnomer, or throwback to simpler times. The chief clerk of the House and the secretary of the Senate are administrators, controlling everything from parliamentary procedure to parking assignments and pages. Still, Snyder found the Senate more appealing. In the Senate, he was in charge of a roughly 250-person staff—doormen, bill room workers, clerks—and a multi-million dollar budget, but there were only half as many members to keep happy. Several of those members recently had moved over from the House, so Snyder knew them well. Snyder liked the camaraderie of the smaller chamber, which at the time was all male. He also liked the fact that his job was safe for four years, instead of two. That security was important. Eventually, he would do well enough for himself that he was able to donate large chunks of what he earned in the Legislature back to taxpayers, but in 1969—with a wife, three teenagers, and a mortgage on his store—that was not yet the case. The Senate job paid Snyder $85 a day during session and $400 a month during the interim.

Insiders considered Snyder's new job to be more powerful than all but the top-level legislators. As secretary, he spent many hours with those top leaders in the Democratic caucus discussing which bills should be advanced and his party's overall strategy. His institutional memory was peerless, and he was a de facto member of leadership.

When the 1969 session ended, Snyder's grocery store was at the tail end of a major remodel intended to double its size before the Memorial Day Weekend tourist rush at the beach—thousands upon thousands of dollars of revenue. To stay on schedule, construction on the Pacific Avenue market was starting early in the morning and ending late in the evening, all while Snyder was in Olympia closing up shop on the session. Snyder wrapped that work up in 10 days. On the morning of Friday, May 22, he was about to check out of his hotel room and head back to Long Beach when his wife called his room:

"The store's on fire and it's bad, real bad."

The hilly, winding 110 miles he faced were among the most mentally difficult he had ever driven. He sped along, praying no one had died and that the damage was not as severe as Bette's call had made it out to be. He envisioned what he would tell any state trooper who pulled him over. "Where do you think you're going, to a fire?" He wondered if he might muster some sense of humor and say, "Yes!"

Firefighters and construction workers team up to douse hotspots as smoke billows out of Sid's Market in Seaview on May 22, 1969. Snyder was working in Olympia at the time, but rushed home as soon as he received the news. *Snyder family photo*

The looks on Sid and Bette Snyder's faces say it all as they sit on boxes of salvaged inventory following the fire. *Snyder family photo*

Firefighters had extinguished the flames by the time Snyder arrived, but his store still was smoldering. The new addition was gutted. A contractor, Joe Gisler, had discovered the fire when he arrived for work. Gisler broke into the store to use the phone but was overcome by the smoke and heat. He collapsed before he could make it back outside. Snyder learned that two men had likely saved the contractor's life by grabbing his arms hard enough to leave bruises and dragging him to safety. They had taken him to the hospital to be treated for smoke inhalation and burns. Snyder surveyed the ruins. Just two walls of his remodel still stood. Bette had already been inside the store to grab the charge accounts, and the insurance adjuster was on site. "You can keep your crew on and you can start tomorrow cleaning up the place and we'll pay you for that," he said. "Hell," Snyder declared, "we're not going to wait until tomorrow; we're going to do it today."

And they did. Everyone began shoveling scorched groceries into Dumpsters, removing what remained of the roof and digging trenches for the in-floor refrigeration system. The shelves were restocked before the store had windows, so Snyder hired someone to stand watch during the few early-morning hours the store was not being worked on. The remodeled and expanded Sid's Market reopened July 3, 1969, the day before the two-lane street out front would be bumper to bumper with traffic coming through town to watch Long Beach's popular fireworks celebration. It was a celebration years earlier Snyder had helped create, and one years later he helped strengthen by drafting legislation to allow the City of Long Beach to use money from lodging taxes to pay off the bonds its had used to build a half-mile long wooden boardwalk west of Long Beach's city center. The legislation was typical Snyder, written with such a narrow scope so it only would apply to the intended purpose: "For cities bordering on the Pacific Ocean with a population greater than 1,000, and for counties in which such cities are located, the uses of the basic 2.0 percent local option hotel/motel tax are expanded to include funding of: 1) special events or festivals, or 2) promotional infrastructures, including an ocean beach boardwalk."

The Snyders pose for a photo inside their market one year after a fire had gutted the store. From left are Sally, Bette, Sid Jr., and Karen. *Sally Snyder Paxton photo*

The above-dunes boardwalk eventually became a popular gathering spot year round—particularly so on the Fourth of July, when the town's population often would quadruple to 6,000 or more.

In January 1970, Snyder was confronted by another fire, this one in the middle of the night at the Tyee Motor Inn in Tumwater where many legislators stayed during session. He awoke to someone pounding on the door of his first-floor room. He put on his pants and stepped outside into the rain as a rapidly spreading blaze wiped out all but 39 of the luxury motel's 209 units. Snyder's room was the second one the fire reached. *The Olympian* reported that one guest staying in the motel's cabanas, separate units hardly affected by the fire, had slept through the excitement and was only discovered on a final sweep by firefighters. Snyder said there was more to the story. The lucky guest was a married legislator, "not to be named," curled up with his girlfriend. "He woke up the next morning, pulled the curtain, and goes, 'What happened?!' He had slept through the whole thing," Snyder said, relishing the tale.

Snyder was in Olympia for the extraordinary 1970 session called by Governor Dan Evans. It was the second time in state history a special session had been held at a time other than immediately following a regular session. Evans' decision was unpopular. Most legislators had full-time jobs outside the Capitol and found it difficult to get away. It would be 10 more years before the state's Constitution was amended to require annual sessions.

Snyder's family was not pleased with the extra time-commitment either. Throughout the years, Bette had grumbled about her spouse's absence, normally taking her frustrations out on paper in the form of droll letters and poetry. Some legislative "widows" gave their spouses an earful when they wandered home for short breaks. Bette composed couplets and essays. One was reprinted in 1970 by Adele Ferguson, the syndicated Capitol columnist for the *Bremerton Sun,* and subsequently picked up in newspapers across the state. Bette wrote:

This is a man whose mind cannot retain a simple grocery list, or remember our wedding anniversary, but if you name any senator or representative of the last thirty years, he can tell you his county, when he first ran for office, how many years he served and probably how many votes he won by. … Small wonder our kids are normal. For years Sid wouldn't let them read children's stories. Instead he'd read to them from the *Congressional Record*. They thought the only time Old Mother Hubbard's cupboard was bare was during a Republican administration. They were quite old before I convinced them the Democrats didn't ALWAYS steal from the rich and give to the poor. … They weren't allowed to argue like other kids. At first sign of a fight, Sid would bang the gavel and act as parliamentarian. Their quarrels always ended up in caucus. … And can he fall asleep like others by counting sheep? No, he calls the Senate roll: Anderson, Atwood, Bailey, Canfield, Connor … The last time he called for anything in his sleep it was for Senator Gordon Walgren. … The other day I thought I'd shake him up so I told him if he didn't start paying more attention to me and less to his Olympia job, I was going to consult a lawyer about a divorce. His reply? "There are any number of good lawyers available, sixteen in the House and seventeen in the Senate."[4]

Snyder never took offense at anything his wife wrote. They were like George Burns and Gracie Allen—they understood each other and had a shtick. They were even more like Mike Nichols and Elaine May, because Sid was not much of a straight man and Bette, to be sure, was no airhead. Sid and Bette called their interplay "our humor," and did not expect those new to their circle to understand it. They never altered their patter so anyone could. Snyder adored his bright and feisty wife, and the feeling was mutual. Nor was Bette's writing doggerel. It had an Ogden Nash quality. Sid shared her slice-of-legislative-life tales with his colleagues and their spouses, who could fully empathize. "It's the luck of the draw with the two of us," Snyder said. "I don't know how I could have found—and 'found' isn't really the right word—a better person for a wife than Bette. Our personalities click or clash or whatever you want to call it."

Bette worked a lot at the store in her husband's absence. The kids did too, especially in the summertime. "They would work a shift, and if we'd get busier than we thought, a lot of times we'd call them back," Snyder said. "I think every legislative session that came along we talked about should I go back or should I not go back? At the same time, the store was growing and we had more employees, so it was easier from that standpoint."

The store's most important employee was Chuck Winn, who began working for Snyder in 1965. He worked nearly every job on his way up to manager, and would remain at Sid's Market for decades. Winn became part of the family, literally, when he married Snyder's oldest daughter, Karen. They later divorced.

Having a quality dedicated employee such as Winn was a godsend. As Winn was rising through the ranks, Snyder branched out into banking and real estate and ended up making millions—something beyond his wildest dreams, especially for a kid from Kelso who worked for a dollar a day at age 12.

Secretary of the Senate Snyder and his assistant, Bill Gleason, perform their duties on the Senate floor in the early 1970s. *Washington State Legislature*

Snyder had a hard time getting a loan from the local branch of the National Bank of Commerce [later Rainier National Bank] for his 1969 store expansion. He needed $100,000, and put his store, its inventory and equipment up for collateral—not to mention his good name. But the Seattle-based bank gave him the runaround. He was not amused. "They kept asking for more information. We'd get those questions answered and then they'd come up with some more. I knew I was going to get the loan, but it went on and on like that."

Meanwhile, bills were coming due on the renovations, and there was no way to pay them. Snyder called his accountant in Longview and connected with First Savings & Loan, which granted him the money within a week. Ever the community-minded businessman, Snyder saw opportunity in his own unhappy experience. He gathered several other local businessmen, and met with them regularly at his home over the next two years to come up with a business plan. Then they applied to the state to charter a bank of their own. The application was approved in 1971, and The Bank of the Pacific, or "Sid's Bank" as locals called it for years, was formed. Within a year, banking experts were touting The Bank of the Pacific as an industry success story. It was a success locally, as well. "When our small businesses were hit by financial turbulence, unlike the typical Wall Street bank, Sid's bank helped figure out a solution and worked with you to get through the rough patch," said Nabiel Shawa, a Long Beach native and the town's former city administrator.

The bank had some rough periods early on, but persevered, then prospered. In 1999, The Bank of the Pacific merged with The Bank of Grays Harbor, and in 2004, Bellingham-based Bank Northwest was brought into the fold. Snyder served as chairman of the bank's board for 25 years, then served as vice-chair after the 1999 merger. By 2013, there were 17 Bank of the Pacific branches serving small communities throughout the region. Corporate headquarters have since shifted from Long Beach to Aberdeen, but a regional office and the original branch remain in Long Beach, at the corner of Pacific Avenue and Sid Snyder Drive.

John McCarthy, right, supervisor of Washington State's Division of Banks, hands Snyder and D. R. Beckman the charter for The Bank of the Pacific in 1971. Beckman was the bank's first president. *Snyder family photo*

The Bank of the Pacific and Sid's Market were just two of the many business enterprises Snyder was involved with over the years. Partly as a tax write-off and partly to help the needy of his community, he bought land immediately west of the bank's Long Beach branch and, with the help of others, built a 34-unit, low-cost housing project for senior citizens. He also built the Edgewater Hotel. In the 1990s, Snyder's business dealings even crossed the Columbia River, when he became partner in a car dealership in Astoria.

Snyder's early years as Senate secretary were busy ones, too, especially compared to the relatively routine final year he had spent as assistant chief clerk. In the special session of 1970—Snyder's first as secretary and his son's senior year at Ilwaco High School—the state departments of Ecology and Social and Health Services were formed. "Ecology," the coming thing, was a new term to Snyder and many others. In the 1972 special session, voters passed the Equal Rights Amendment and I-276, a landmark public records law that Snyder believed forever changed the face of the Legislature—for the worse. After the law was implemented, "a lot of people didn't want to run because they had to disclose so much of their personal net worth. I think personally the caliber of legislators went down after the passage."

Nineteen-seventy-two also was the year of one of Snyder's personal highlights. That July, he and 20-year-old Sid Jr.—now a student at Lewis and Clark College in Portland—flew to Miami Beach, Florida, for the Democratic National Convention. It was not necessarily the trip that made the event so memorable, but the fact that both father and son were delegates. Sid Jr. was one of five alternates, but he was selected to attend as a delegate at the last minute after one delegate took sick and ended up in a Longview hospital. The Snyders, the only father-son team in attendance, were at the delegation to support their home-state man, Henry M. "Scoop" Jackson. The popular United States senator was making the first of two consecutive attempts to win the Democratic presidential nomination. Jackson had been eliminated by the time it was Washington's time to vote, so the delegation cast its votes for eventual nominee, South Dakota Senator George McGovern. McGovern won the nomination with 57 percent of the delegate vote, but was walloped in November by President Richard Nixon.

The '72 convention was the second Snyder had attended as a delegate. The first had been four years earlier in Chicago, where he was the only Hubert Humphrey supporter in the delegation. The third came in 1980 in New York; and the fourth was in 2004 in Boston. In Boston, Snyder was on hand at the FleetCenter as a largely unknown U.S. Senate candidate from Illinois, Barack Obama, gave a now legendary keynote speech that catapulted him onto the national stage. "That was the first time I'd ever heard of Obama," Snyder said. When Obama captured the Democratic presidential nomination four years later, it brought Snyder to tears. He never thought he would see a black man accomplish such a feat. Snyder flashed back to a moment when he was a child in Kelso, delivering clothes in a wagon. A successful haberdasher had told him then: "Son, you can be anything you want to be."

Snyder faced the first of several health scares in 1973. During a routine visit to his family doctor, he casually mentioned a swollen testicle and in nothing flat was headed to Astoria for surgery. The lump was cancerous, so Snyder made visits to Portland for radium-based radiation therapy. The radiation kept the cancer from spreading, but doctors later told him the radium also had damaged his lungs and his heart's aortic valve. Snyder had the valve replaced with a cow valve 21 years later after he collapsed at his Seattle condominium. The valve-replacement surgery took place in June 1994. Snyder was in the hospital for a week, and left on the 17th, the same day police chased O.J. Simpson's

Snyder attended the 1968 Democratic National Convention in Chicago as a Hubert Humphrey supporter—the only one in his delegation. Snyder also attended Democratic National Conventions in 1972, 1980, and 2004. *Snyder family photo*

white Ford Bronco over the highways of Southern California. It was no surprise that Bette found humor in her husband's rather serious procedure. She wrote:

There are however subtle changes in him now and he has taken on traits normally associated with cattle. His skin is becoming white, leathery and hairy. And although he was always quite docile I sometimes find him wandering aimlessly in the tall grass in the dunes. He won't eat beef and eats lots of green food. He chews each mouthful a very long time which drives me to distraction and makes eating out embarrassing. … Oh yes, I should tell you he bought me a bell to wear around my neck. He said I'm easier to find when I'm wearing it. Imagine, as we drive by Rose Ranch he gazes longingly at his comrades in the fields, he used to look at me like that. And yet for all my consternation I am very glad that they didn't use the pig valve. I'd rather be called Clara Bell than Miss Piggy.[5]

Health issues rarely affected Snyder's performance at work—at any of his jobs. And his performance at one job never seemed to suffer for the existence of the other. In 1974, in fact, Snyder was named the Pacific County Democrat of the Year and the Washington State Grocer of the Year. The latter award was given, in part, due to testimony Snyder had made the previous spring at a U.S. Senate Commerce Committee hearing. When Snyder, who had flown to Washington, D.C., on his own dime, finished testifying on the complicated issue of food surveillance, he approached Senator Philip Hart of Michigan, the committee chair, and asked him not to forget what he had said on behalf of independent small-town grocers. The white-bearded Democrat, widely known as the conscience of the Senate, turned to Snyder and asked, "How could we?"[6]

Snyder's core political beliefs were simple: Combine common sense and cross-party compromise and you will get the best outcome. His popularity over the years was no doubt linked to those two values, although he at times could be a strong party loyalist, a fact best showcased during the 1976 gubernatorial race. Snyder's preferred candidate that year was Seattle Mayor Wes Uhlman, an Aberdeen High School graduate and former state senator. Yet when Uhlman narrowly lost in the primary to political newcomer Dixy Lee Ray, a peculiar but popular marine biologist born in Tacoma, Snyder jumped in to help although he never had met her. Ray went on to beat King County Executive John Spellman in the general election to become the first female governor in Washington history. Statewide, she received 53 percent of the vote to Spellman's 44 percent. In Pacific County, where Snyder and Bob Bailey had co-chaired her campaign, her win was more decisive—Ray: 61 percent, Spellman: 36 percent.

It took only one term for the hip-shooting Ray to fall out of favor with the press, the public, and her own party, but not before she played a role in two memorable incidents that directly involved Snyder. The first came during a luncheon during the 1977 session as the last-to-arrive Snyder moved toward the only remaining seat, which happened to be to next to the governor. Snyder's long-standing habit of slightly lifting his seat up before he settled into it hurt him this time, as he unknowingly placed the leg of his chair on top of Ray's beloved poodle, Jacques. "There was a horrendous howling from Jacques, who was picked up and soothed by the governor while Snyder looked as if he'd just been sentenced to Washington state's version of Devil's Island,"[7] Adele Ferguson wrote in her column. A short time later, Snyder was the subject of a Senate spoof. A pretend resolution, recited with solemnity, cited the governor's new plans to cordon off the

The Snyder brothers—Rufus, Sid, Vic, and Floyd—pose with mom in May 1973.

Long Beach Peninsula for use as a maximum-security prison. Further, she now planned to alleviate Washington's school-funding crisis by levying a 65 percent business-and-occupation tax upon grocers.

Later that session, during a going-away party in the Senate for Bob Bailey, whom Ray had appointed to the Utilities and Transportation Commission, the governor had Snyder pose for a photo in which he knelt while Ray commanded Jacques to bite his leg.

Governor Dixy Lee Ray jokingly instructs her poodle Jacques to bite Snyder's leg during a going-away party for Senator Bob Bailey in 1977. Earlier that year, Snyder had inadvertently placed the leg of his chair down on top of the dog. *Washington State Legislature*

Snyder's respect for Ray hit an all-time low in April 1980, when two of the state's rising-star Democrats, Co-Speaker of the House John Bagnariol of Renton and Senate Majority Leader Gordon Walgren of Bremerton, were arrested on federal racketeering charges. Together with lobbyist Patrick Gallagher, the pair had been charged with conspiring with undercover FBI agents posing as California businessmen to ease gambling laws in the state in exchange for part of the profits. In October, Gallagher was found guilty on all 14 charges against him; Bagnariol was guilty on nine of his 11, and Walgren on three of 13. Each man spent roughly two years at the Federal Prison Camp in Lompoc, California, although Walgren ultimately won the right to resume his law practice and had two of his three convictions thrown out on appeal.

At the time of their arrests, Bagnariol and Walgren had been on the verge of declaring their candidacies for higher office. Bagnariol had planned to challenge Ray for governor, while Walgren—a former Kitsap County prosecutor—was gunning to become the state's attorney general. Many people, including the defendants, believed the Washington State Patrol, acting under the direction of Governor Ray, conducted a politically inspired investigation in concert with the FBI.

Snyder never wavered from the belief that his good friend Walgren, whom he had known for more than a dozen years, was framed. In fact, it was Snyder who talked Walgren out of resigning as majority leader shortly after the indictments had been handed down. "I told him that if he was convicted, he could resign at that time but if he resigned now and was acquitted—as we all expected—there would be no way for him to get it back."[8]

Decades later, mere mention of the "Gamscam" case still fired Snyder up. He owned a copy of the trial transcripts and had read every page. He had thrown a welcome-home party for Walgren at the Tyee when he was paroled in 1984. He believed his friend was innocent. "*Absolutely*. I know him so well. We had dinner a couple times a week. I was around him. He wouldn't even sell a ticket in his office for a fundraiser or anything like that. I'm just convinced. There is a crime there and that's that the FBI conjured up these stories. Every time the FBI accused Gordy of taking money, I knew he didn't take money. I would bet my life on it. But if you're on the jury who do you believe, a politician or an FBI agent?"

Walgren said the steadfast support of Snyder, and that of others, including Adele Ferguson, often helped get him through the long nights in Lompoc: "If you don't have friends, you don't have anything. Sid was always one of my very best friends in that regard. Sid was never afraid to express his views on [Gamscam] publicly. That takes a lot of guts."

If Governor Ray was indeed involved, and had hoped to gain a political advantage from Bagnariol and Walgren's fall from grace, it did not work. Ray was defeated in the 1980 primary by Senator Jim McDermott, who lost in the general election to John Spellman, the King County executive Ray had defeated in 1976.

Seven ▪ Sedentary S.O.B.

ONE OF THE LAST VESTIGES OF WASHINGTON's horse-and-buggy Legislature—biennial sessions—disappeared in 1980, thanks to approval of a constitutional amendment that authorized annual sessions. There would be no more need to cover clocks to finish business, a political maneuver done by earlier legislatures that eventually was ruled unconstitutional. Even-numbered years now would feature 60-day sessions. Odd-numbered, budget-tackling years would be 105 days. Such annual meetings had become commonplace across the United States, and special sessions had been the norm in Olympia throughout the 1970s. Too much business, too little time.

The change officially increased the amount of time Sid Snyder—then known in political circles as "The 50th Senator"—was required to spend away from home. He was up for the new time commitment but also believed that annual sessions, together with the passage of the public records act eight years earlier and the increasing maliciousness of campaigns, further weakened the legislative talent pool. What established professional—a doctor, lawyer, CPA or grocer—would be willing, or able, to abandon a prosperous job for a large chunk of the year simply to serve the public in a fishbowl for relatively low compensation? Finding those types of people was not easy, and Snyder believed the Legislature, not to mention the taxpayers, suffered. Though his office was not an elected one, Snyder was one of the rare exceptions whose personal situation afforded him an opportunity to serve in Olympia and maintain success in his "real" job. His market was doing well under the daily guidance of manager Chuck Winn; The Bank of the Pacific and his other business ventures were succeeding, and

Lieutenant Governor John Cherberg speaks with a page as he and Snyder walk through the halls of the Senate in 1981. As Cherberg grew older, he leaned more and more on Snyder for assistance in presiding over the Senate. *Washington State Legislature*

he and Bette recently had become empty nesters. Sid Jr. was an up-and-coming attorney in Seattle, Karen had married Winn and was operating a private preschool in Long Beach for three- and four-year-olds, and Sally had moved to Bellevue to work as a legal secretary and attend college. The Snyder children all benefitted from a deal their parents had made them regarding higher education. The parents agreed to pay half of each kid's tuition, books, and room and board, and the kids were responsible for everything else. Snyder believed that making his children earn their way in life—just as he had done—was the way to go, even if he had the means for them not to have to do so. All the children had worked at the store throughout their high school years and even earlier, and Sid Jr. and Karen also worked at the store during their college breaks.

Snyder was on hand in 1981 to witness one of the most dramatic events in Senate history. As Snyder began his 13th year as the body's secretary, Democrats held a slim 25-24 majority with Ted Bottiger serving as their leader. One month after the session began, on Friday the 13th of February, Senator Peter von Reichbauer shocked the state by switching parties at a hastily called press conference in which he said he no longer could relate to his fellow Democrats. Von Reichbauer's switch handed Republicans the majority, bumped Bottiger to minority leader, and elevated Walla Walla Republican Jeannette Hayner to majority leader—the first woman in history to hold the position. Snyder was stunned by von Reichbauer's decision. "It threw everything into an upheaval. Peter is a hard person to understand. I consider [him] a friend, but he's a great manipulator. I think he wanted a certain office." Although his party no longer was in the majority, Snyder was asked to remain in his position. Von Reichbauer was one of those fighting for Snyder to remain secretary.

Snyder remained friends with von Reichbauer, who survived a recall

Snyder's doings in Olympia often became the subject for editorial cartoons, especially in his hometown of Long Beach. Don Cole, *Chinook Observer*

Snyder receives a cozy ride on a trip to Singapore in 1982. *Snyder family photo*

effort and continued to serve the 30th District as a senator until 1992, when he left to become a King County councilman. In fact, it was von Reichbauer who during the mid-1980s orchestrated visits to Long Beach for several Seattle sports stars, including Seahawks quarterback Jim Zorn and Hall of Fame wide receiver Steve Largent. Each came to visit the Snyders—big-time supporters of Seattle's professional sports teams—and to fish.

"I can remember Zorn with a pair of dairy overalls on and no shirt on underneath. And Bette said, 'What are all those red spots?' Well, that's where he had gotten sacked on Sunday. And then Largent and his wife came and they had their six-week-old son with them and put him in a dresser drawer upstairs in their room." Governor Spellman, an avid fisherman, came to visit the Snyders during his time in office, too. Sid and Bette turned their house over to John, his wife, Lois, and a few others and went to stay in a cabin they owned nearby. One evening, when the Spellman group returned from dinner, they realized they had locked the key inside the Snyder house. After an attempt to pick the lock with his credit card failed, the governor grabbed a ladder that was being used by painters working on the home, leaned it against a gutter running along a flat section of the roof, climbed up and crawled inside through an unlocked window. Snyder and Spellman often joked about the incident, and pondered what might have happened had police shown up. Spellman said his response would have been, "Hi, I'm the governor."

A similarly humorous story occurred around the same period when Senator Dan McDonald, the Republican floor leader, popped into Sid's Market one day in July 1985 as he and his sons were beginning a month-long bicycle trip down the coast to the Mexican border. "We got there and I went in to see if Sid was there by chance," McDonald said. "Sure enough, there he was behind the counter checking groceries." Snyder left the checkstand to pose for a pre-adventure photo with the McDonalds outside in front of his store's sign. The sign was advertising a sale on turkey. "Sid claimed that the 'turkey' above our heads was a description of me, not an ad for meat," McDonald said. "I never did get even with him for that."

When Republican Senator Dan McDonald, right, and sons began their bicycle trip to the Mexican border at Seaview in July 1985, Sid posed with the family underneath his market's sign. In front of Snyder are Tod and Evan McDonald. *Dan McDonald*

On another occasion, when Representative Georgette Valle and her husband visited Snyder in Long Beach, Valle called the only cab in town. Once inside, she asked the driver if he knew who his state representatives were. The driver had no clue. He had no reason to stay informed politically, he told Valle, because at election time he always took his ballot down to Sid's Market and had the owner make his selections for him.

The issue of Snyder running for office again surfaced in 1984 when Bottiger encouraged him to run for the 19th District Senate seat vacated by Aberdeen Republican J.T. Quigg. *The Seattle Times* liked Snyder's chances, calling him "one of the Senate's best-loved figures ... the Legislature's resident historian and a wonderful storyteller who recounts quips and anecdotes from lawmakers dating back to the 1950s."[1] Snyder told *The Times*, "I think the Democrats need me. I think they need the viewpoint of a businessman."[2] Snyder eventually had second thoughts, and decided he was content working behind the scenes.

It would take four more years—nearly a quarter-century after Governor Rosellini had cornered him in a car and asked him to run against a member of the notorious 1963 House coalition—until timing and opportunity combined to present a scenario intriguing enough to entice Snyder to give elected politics a try.

That series of events began in November 1987, during a special election in which Linda Smith, a movement conservative from Vancouver, won a vacated 18th District seat to give Republicans a majority in the Senate. The Republicans announced they were going to put their own man, Tacoma attorney Gordon Golob, in the top administrative post for the 1988 session. The decision signaled an end to Snyder's 19 years as secretary of the Senate, but he was not yet out the door. Nor was 77-year-old John Cherberg. But in recent years, as the lieutenant governor's hearing and mind had begun to fail, Cherberg had leaned heavily on Snyder to help preside over the Senate. Snyder never spoke about Cherberg's decline, but others did. "At times, Snyder can be heard prompting Cherberg with the precise wording of motions,"[3] stated one Associated Press article in December 1987. Augie Mardesich, who had moved from the House to the Senate, believed Snyder was invaluable: "He knew all the internal operations. He knew who was where on most issues. He really had his finger on it."[4]

Republicans also knew how important Snyder was, not only to Cherberg and the Senate, but also to the institution. They did not want to see him go, so they developed a proposal to keep Snyder on staff at his current pay of $6,200 a month as Golob's assistant and assign him to help Cherberg. Snyder worked Cherberg's final session in 1988, and then resigned in May. He was offered the opportunity to stick around, but believed he was no longer needed. "I wouldn't have been worth my weight in salt," he said.

Snyder returned to Long Beach and soon decided he would throw his hat into the ring to replace Cherberg, retiring after a 32-year, national-record run as lieutenant governor. Who better to run the Senate than the person who had been doing it, de facto as it may have been, for the past couple sessions? Snyder had learned a lot from his fast friend. "We

Sid and Bette hosted a party—featuring an ice-sculpture centerpiece—
at the Tyee Motor Inn in Tumwater. The hosts are pictured with Betty
and John Cherberg. *Snyder family photo*

had much in common," Snyder said, "humble beginnings, grocery back-grounds, both married 'Bettys,' both had two daughters and one son, both Democrats and both were dedicated to the legislative process." Cherberg, no surprise, touted Snyder as the best candidate for the job.

He had traveled with Snyder wives in tow, on trade missions to Italy, Japan, Russia, and Scotland. He knew what Snyder was made of. "Often, we would travel for 24 hours or longer to arrive at a destination, and we would all be exhausted," Snyder said. "Most of us could fall into bed, but John and Betty would be met by some excited dignitary and would be required to go to dinner. They would take five minutes to freshen up and graciously join their hosts."

Snyder's campaign fliers declared him the "Best Choice for Lieutenant Governor," and highlighted his years of working with Cherberg, his business experience, and his community involvement. "Sid Snyder has established his credentials as an active parliamentarian and expert in the

Snyder gave it his all in his bid for lieutenant governor. He even had campaign bibs made, which he and Bette wore to the Pacific County Democrats' Crab Feed. *Snyder family photo*

legislative process," the flier read. Despite his qualifications, Snyder made a rookie campaign mistake that sunk his chances: He waited too long to publicly declare his candidacy. By the time his hat was in the ring, several other Democrats—including Senators George Fleming, Brad Owen, and Nita Rinehart—were well into their campaigns, and many key organizations already had handed out endorsements. "I lost out on that opportunity. I got around the state a little and I had most of the Senate members backing me, which I thought would be a plus, and it would have been. But I didn't have any support. The polls said I had 2 percent or something like that. It was a long thing to overcome." Snyder never bothered to file. Fleming, a former University of Washington football star like Cherberg, earned the Democrats' nomination but lost in the general election to personable Joel Pritchard, a charter member of the Evans Republicans.

It appeared an end had come to the 62-year-old Snyder's 40-year Capitol story. That was fine with happy-at-home Bette, who chose to commemorate Sid's homecoming in a letter to her husband:

"It was time, finally, to plan our future together, and oh, the preparations I made. With high expectations, I dieted, primped, permed and burned the fuzzy robe. I stopped looking frowsy and frazzled. I subscribed to *Bon Appetit*; planned delicious dinners. Always a romantic, I envisioned long, lazy evenings watching the sun set, sipping fine wine by candlelight, recapturing the loving days we once had."[5]

Later in the letter, written a year after Snyder left the Senate, reality wife realizes romantic wife's expectations may have been a bit lofty:

"What happened to that young, eager, sleek dark-haired guy, the winsome one who laughed a lot, was fit and flexible, a sexy guy full of charm and confidence, the guy as happy as Willard Scott? Who, I asked, is this quiet portly guy with gray at the temples, the sedentary, S.O.B. couch potato who returned? You went away a young dad and returned a grandfather. Could I handle this transformation?"[6]

After leaving the Senate in May 1988 for what appeared to be good, Snyder returned home to help out around his store. Here, he bags groceries for a customer. *Snyder family photo*

Bette decided she could work on things:

> "I think we can find a compromise and get used to each other again. So, Sid, put your feet on the furniture, leave your newspapers on the floor. After serving forty years in Olympia you deserve the good life. And lucky you, you get to share it with me. WELCOME HOME AT LAST. Our love is here to stay."[7]

Although Bette's letter paints the picture of a conflicted woman, the Snyders' love never was in jeopardy of heading south, for the winter or any other time of year. But Bette knew there always was a chance her husband would head northeast again. Especially if his fever for Olympia ever returned, which it did in August 1990. After a lengthy battle with a blood disorder, Democratic Senator Arlie DeJarnatt of Longview, Snyder's longtime friend, died at age 67. Earlier in the year, his health declining, DeJarnatt had mailed a letter to his 19th District constituents, updating them on his condition and naming Snyder as one of the people he wished to succeed him if illness forced him to resign. DeJarnatt also told several newspapers Snyder would be the logical choice for his seat.

Snyder did not have much time to ponder whether he should fulfill his late friend's request. Due to the proximity of DeJarnatt's death to the printing of absentee ballots for that September's primary election, a special filing period had to be scheduled for the week DeJarnatt died even before his funeral took place. Snyder realized the situation was sensitive. He remembered Julia Butler Hansen's statement to the media in 1960 when she was asked if she would be running to fill Russell Mack's congressional seat. Out of respect, she had said she would wait until after the funeral to discuss the matter. Circumstances did not afford Snyder that option, so he reluctantly called DeJarnatt's widow, Donna, to seek her opinion. She knew of the time crunch, having been told about it by Secretary of State Ralph Munro. Donna DeJarnatt told Snyder to file, and even volunteered to be his unofficial campaign manager. At Arlie DeJarnatt's end-of-the-week memorial service, Snyder said goodbye to his friend the best way he knew. Using the Latin phrase that adjourned every legislative session, he said, "Sine die, Arlie."

Snyder was appointed to fill the last few months of DeJarnatt's term and then ran in his own right. He was heavily favored to beat his one Democratic opponent, Aberdeen Mayor O'Dean Williamson, in the September primary. Williamson had done a successful job running his city of 18,000, but had nowhere near the name recognition and reputation Snyder enjoyed in the sprawling four-county district. As local newspaper editorial boards began handing out endorsements, it was clear who their favorite was. An editorial cartoon in *The Chinook Observer* featured Snyder driving a steamroller with the words "OLYMPIA EXPRESS" written on the drum. The *Observer* later told its readers, "Send Sid to Olympia. You'll be glad you did."[8] Coming from Snyder's hometown, those endorsements were somewhat expected. But non-Long Beach papers were firmly behind Snyder, too. *The Daily World,* in Williamson's hometown, was boldest in

Arlie DeJarnatt during his early days in the House of Representatives. *Washington State Legislature*

its belief in Snyder: "For the record, the two candidates agree on most everything. For the record, Snyder is going to win."[9]

Snyder appreciated the media's support but had learned from his abortive run for lieutenant governor. There would be no "what ifs" this time around. He was going to work hard and run this campaign the right way. To Bette's chagrin, that included asking his family to pound the pavement with him. Doorbelling proved an

Snyder's hometown newspaper obviously liked his chances for success in the 1990 election. Don Cole, *Chinook Observer*

eye-opening experience for all. During one early stop in a rough section of Aberdeen, Bette turned to her husband and asked if they could go to a better neighborhood. "This is where the Democrats live," he told her, and she dutifully knocked on the door. A young man came to the door in nothing but his skivvies. She told him why she was there. And he said, "Who's he running against?" She had balked at saying, "It's your mayor" in case he liked Williamson. But she did. The guy shot back, "Oh, I wouldn't vote for that S.O.B.! How does your husband feel about gun control?" She didn't have a clue. Well, the man said, "I don't care how he feels on gun control, I'd never vote for that S.O.B. mayor."

The visit was awkward for another reason: "I didn't know where to look because I wear bifocals and if I look through the bottom it looks like I'm looking at the bottom of his shorts," Bette said. "And if I put my head down and look through the top it kind of looks the same way."

The Snyders probably could have done without the doorbelling. Sid walked away with 74 percent of the vote. In his home county of Pacific, he received six times as many votes as Williamson. Snyder advanced to November's general election, where he nearly tripled the vote count of his Republican challenger, Carolyn Feasey. Snyder ran unchallenged for the next decade.

There was no mistaking who Bette Snyder's favorite candidate for office was as she and Sid walked the boardwalk at Long Beach in 1990. *Snyder family photo*

Eight ▪ Senator

Sid likes his new challenge
He's having a ball
When he's called "Senator"
He feels ten feet tall.

He's off making speeches
Sometimes near, mostly far
The most I see of him
Is in the car.

He makes me go with him
Which isn't much fun
I'd rather be shopping
If you don't mind the pun.

Yes, the District's his life now
That's plain to see
Before the election
It used to be ME.

From "Senator's Wife's Lament" by Bette Snyder, January 1991

Fʀᴏᴍ ᴛʜᴇ ᴇᴀʀʟɪᴇꜱᴛ ᴅᴀʏꜱ, the path from Pacific County to the Capitol was not an easy one.

J.L. "Joel" Brown was the first man from the coast-to-hills county nominated to the original territorial Legislature—a nine-member assembly that convened February 27, 1854, in a two-story dry goods store on Olympia's wagon-rutted Main Street. Brown was one of only 61 of the county's 150 white men deemed eligible to hold office. So it was no surprise that his was the only name on the ballot. Brown set off for Olympia before a vote could even be held. Willard R. Espy, whose family was among the founders of the Pacific County community of Oysterville, later wrote that Brown had been homesteading on the Palix River when he began his journey, "and he tramped, and he canoed, and he fell through hollow hills of blackberry bushes, and he ran out of shot, and he smashed his leg between two floating logs, and he wore himself to such a frazzle that he came stumbling back to his cabin and fell on his bunk and died."[1]

Long Beach pioneer Jehu Scudder replaced Brown on the ballot, and lived long enough to get elected. He began his trek northeast through the wild Willapa country in early February. Though his name appeared several times in that year's *House Journal*, Scudder never made it to Olympia, either. He had chosen to try to follow Indian foot trails the entire way but died somewhere en route nine days before the session was to open. Indians retrieved his body, as the story goes, and returned it to Long Beach. Scudder was buried on his own land claim just outside town. The *Journal* officially recognized Scudder's death March 2.

Scudder's replacement, Henry Fiester, made it to Olympia, was sworn into office March 30, then hit the local watering hole with several of his new colleagues. Espy wrote that Fiester was "sitting in a saloon, having a nip to restore his strength, when he fell off his chair and was dead before he hit the floor. The newspaper said [the] next day he had been called from time to eternity by a stroke of apoplexy, but everyone knew the trip to Olympia killed him."[2] Eventually, a man named James Clark Strong was voted to be the county's representative. Strong served from the middle of

Reporters and photographers greeted Snyder in the parking garage
below the Legislative Building after Snyder was appointed to fill the seat
of late Senator Arlie DeJarnatt. *Louie Balukoff*

April until the session adjourned May 1 and went on to serve as a Union officer in the Civil War.

By the time he took office, Sid Snyder had been the Legislature's unofficial historian for decades. He knew all about Brown, Scudder, Fiester, and Strong. But, more important, he had been a supporting character in several more memorable stories that form the lore of the Legislature—Julia Butler Hansen's near-miss to become the first lady speaker; the coup that ousted John O'Brien; the night they threatened to swear in Dan Evans early; the redistricting face-offs between Bob Greive and Slade Gorton. Snyder had no trouble getting to Olympia for his first day on the job, and no trouble obtaining a leadership role once he got there. In 1991, his Senate colleagues elected him caucus chair over two formidable opponents—Pat McMullen, who once had worked as an assistant attorney general under Gorton; and Mike Kreidler, a future congressman and state insurance commissioner.

Together, McMullen and Kreidler had held elective office for more than 20 years; Snyder had begun working at the Capitol before either of the men had reached second grade. In that sense, he was the most experienced freshman in legislative history.

The Senate majority's new number two man was 64 years old, and had run the body and many of its meetings for years. He was regarded an outstanding listener whose gift for storytelling could quickly transform a contentious gathering into a complaisant one. The first freshman caucus chair in state history also entered office with a reputation as an infectious worker: a man who showed up early, stayed late, and hardly took a break. "He worked all the time," said Nyla Wood, who worked with Snyder in various capacities for 25 years. "Working is what he loved most. That was Sid. He would leave Olympia late on Friday night, get back to Long Beach in time to check out the day's cash registers, and, when called for, turn around and come right back for a Saturday session." When she became Snyder's assistant, Wood found it difficult to manage the senator's calendar, not only because of his work ethic, but also because he was so congenial. "He had so many friends who wanted to stop by and see him all the time. Friends who just wanted to come in and chat, even though his schedule was full from early morning until he left at night. Even if someone wasn't scheduled, Sid would just wave them in."

Based on her first experience with the man, Wood should have known what she was getting into. Forty years old and new to Olympia, Wood had nervously climbed the Capitol steps to Snyder's third-floor office on Friday, January 7, 1972, three days before the start of that year's special session. The Senate secretary told her there were no jobs available but that he would keep her in mind if anything came up. And it did. At 2 p.m. Sunday, Snyder phoned Wood and told her a position had opened in the Senate workroom.

"When would you like me to start?"

"Right now."

Snyder took office as a senator at a time when state political leadership was perceived as weak. "Capitol Asks: Where Are Leaders?" read a headline in *The Seattle Times* that year. The story that ran below it provided an answer based on interviews with anonymity-requesting business lobbyists, campaign professionals, welfare advocates, and legislators: "There aren't many."[4]

Snyder's political theory was a simple one. Listen and be willing to compromise. He often repeated a saying he first heard spoken by Joel Pritchard during their days in the House: "You can get more done if you don't care who gets credit for it." A legislator's constituents must come above all else, Snyder believed, not because they may vote you out of office if you do otherwise, but because they are your people, you live among them, and they put you in office to help further their interests. Those interests were wide in Snyder's district, which included all of Pacific and Wahkiakum counties, as well as parts of Cowlitz and Grays Harbor. Snyder also would help those outside his legislative boundaries. In Grays Harbor, for example,

Snyder's election to the Senate was a proud moment for himself and his family.
From left, Sid Jr., Sally, Karen, Bette, and Sid document the occasion
with a photo on the rostrum. *Snyder family photo*

Aberdeen was the only one of the sister cities of Aberdeen and Hoquiam that was in his district. "But when someone called me from Hoquiam, I didn't tell them to call someone else," Snyder always said, "I took care of it."

In 1991, Snyder's rural counties were struggling. Recent federal regulations enacted to protect the northern spotted owl had dramatically limited the amount of forest lands available to be logged. As a result, a way of life for thousands of residents of towns in Snyder's blue-collar district—from Aberdeen to Ilwaco, Oakville to Longview—disappeared overnight. *The Seattle Times* declared that if such an "epidemic of distress were hitting thousands of men, women and children and the major businesses in one of our metropolitan areas, it would be the heart-tugging top story on television and in the rest of the news media. But all this went without much news play."[5]

Snyder was not necessarily anti-owl, but there was no doubt he was pro-logger, and he knew those jobs were not going to return any time soon. "What would happen if all the spotted owls were to die?" he wondered. "I don't think there would be anything crucial there. But if you completely stopped logging, what would it do?" He and other members whose citizenry was affected pushed legislation that granted millions of dollars to the communities hit hardest by the logging restrictions. The money helped pay for displaced workers to be retrained, receive extended unemployment benefits and mortgage help, and more. Snyder said he hoped the opportunities would help people "reach out and pull themselves up by their bootstraps."[6] When problems were discovered with the Employment Security Department's implementation of that so-called "Bootstraps Bill," Snyder fought to make sure those who needed help were unaffected by the problems. "[The people] cannot be allowed to fall victim to bureaucratic red tape," he said "It would be the worst sort of cruel irony if the people who need the help the most were not allowed to get it."[7] Within two years, some 2,000 displaced timber workers had received training at various vocational schools and community colleges. Snyder attended many of those graduation ceremonies. Also in 1991, Snyder fought for $450,000 for an environmental impact study on how to control invasive spartina grass in Willapa Bay, which was crowding out the habitat of native species and clogging estuaries. Environmental groups were not pleased with Snyder, but his constituents certainly were.

Of the dozens of sessions he had been a part of, Snyder said the 1991 assembly was the quietest he had ever seen because it was overshadowed by war in the Persian Gulf. He told *The Olympian* in February, "It's always been the Legislature that's the most important thing that's happening. But this time it's secondary. The war is in your front yard, your living room every day, and I think that has quite a chilling effect. There just seems to be a pall over the place that we haven't had in past sessions."[8]

On the last day of the 105-day session, Snyder's peers voted him "Savviest Freshman." One day earlier, he had earned the unofficial title of "Least-Savvy Husband" thanks to an erroneous report in *The Oregonian* announcing that the Washington State Legislature had adjourned. An

Senator Snyder's influence in Pacific County was without question. Here he is seated at the head of the table while Governor Booth Gardner gives a speech during the 68th annual Pacific County Democrats' Crab Feed in 1992. Congresswoman Jolene Unsoeld is seated at far left. *The Daily World*

Oregonian subscriber in Long Beach was dumbfounded by the article and decided to send her husband a terse fax: "Where are you?"

During the 1992 elections, Democrats wrestled the majority in the Senate for the first time since 1987 and maintained a strong majority in the House. They also had the governorship, thanks to former congressman Mike Lowry's narrow win over the state's sitting attorney general, Ken Eikenberry. Snyder again was elected caucus chair, while Marc Gaspard was chosen majority leader. As his fellow Democrats were celebrating their majority status, Snyder was taking into account the feelings of the minority party. "The problems we face are not just Democratic problems," he told one reporter, "and I hope the Republicans will be involved in the process. I hope we will have a five-corners approach (the two caucuses in each house and the governor) in solving our problems."[9]

The 1993 session's hot-button topics included gun control and what to do about a potential $2 billion budget deficit. In light of that shortfall and the likely need for new taxes, Snyder and his allies took some heat over his proposals to grant tax breaks. In one such bill, Snyder sought to exempt from the business-and-occupation tax fish caught outside state waters. His goal was to help his constituents. He felt that without that exemption fish typically processed at The Ilwaco Fish Company, located at the Port of Ilwaco on the north end of the Columbia River's mouth, would instead be processed in Oregon. Snyder's belief was that the state stood to gain from the move not only by keeping workers employed, but also by the ability to assess the state fish tax on the processed fish.

Snyder was all for granting at least one more tax break in 1993, this one to a steel mill called Nucor, which was considering a Cowlitz County site as a location for a high-tech mill that would bring 450 family-wage jobs. Although that tax break also had the support of Governor Lowry, the mill never came. Snyder even drew some rare heat from his fellow Democrats late in the session, when he expressed reservations about a bill that would give the state a new health care system. The bill had been the Legislature's top priority, but the caucus chair felt it was too hard on small businesses such as his own. Amendments eventually appeased Snyder, and the Washington Health Services Act passed, mandating universal health coverage for all Washingtonians. However, major portions of the act were repealed two years later.

The 1993 regular session was followed by a short special session that ended with a shouting match between Snyder and Spokane Republican Jim West, who was angry because an amendment he had proposed had been "trashed" by the Democrats. "I think this Senate should be ashamed of itself,"[10] West said, pointing a finger at the Democrats. When West was ruled out of order by the Senate president, he stood up and shouted again. Snyder took issue:

"I'm not a damn bit ashamed. You people should be ashamed."[11] Snyder later told a reporter, "Sometimes you've got to do that."[12]

Snyder served as Democratic caucus chair for two more sessions, earning a reputation, at least according to *The News Tribune* in Tacoma, as a master of "hanging paper, the art of adding unrelated measures on to other bills, and the deal-brokering that happens at the end of each session."[13] During this period, he jumped head-first into an effort to find an alternate use for a 1,600-acre site in Grays Harbor County that was home to a pair of unfinished nuclear power plants. The 500-foot-tall concrete cooling towers were remnants of the Washington Public Power Supply System's ill-fated push to add five nuclear power plants to the Northwest power grid. Though the site on Fuller Hill at Satsop near Elma was outside the boundaries of Snyder's legislative district, its redevelopment was one of his top goals. For him, job creation always was a priority, and any revenue produced from the Satsop location would benefit his district, too. Two decades earlier, when construction on the towers had commenced, Snyder believed nuclear energy might be that job- and revenue-producer. He did not believe that any longer. "I felt, gosh, we're going to need the electricity and I was all for it. But it turned out to be a boondoggle. It hurt the state in other ways because [the subsequent default of WPPSS] meant that any subdivision in the state, any city or county, water district, sewer district that went to sell their bonds, they got charged more for them because we had a poor record."

Snyder attended meetings and pushed legislation that helped turn the site into the Satsop Development Park, eventually home to high-tech businesses looking to take advantage of the park's exceptional infrastructure. Snyder even met with a trio of Grays Harbor natives who were debating the pros and cons of opening a tech company in such a rural area. He offered an emotional plea as to why they should build in Satsop: "Because your fathers and grandfathers took those same types of risks to build what Grays Harbor became, and now it's your turn."[14]

The company, a call center named SafeHarbor Technology, opened at Satsop in 1998 and two years later employed more than 200 people. SafeHarbor also gained the backing of Governor Gary Locke, who had taken office in 1997. Locke's brother-in-law—in a move that later drew some scrutiny—even became SafeHarbor's chief financial officer. Locke latched onto the company, running it up the political flagpole as an example of the type of high-tech economic development projects he felt could find their way from Puget Sound to Poverty Central. At the time, roughly 20 percent of Grays Harbor County residents lived below the federal poverty level of $16,540 for a family of four. To help move SafeHarbor along, Snyder sponsored legislation granting a $1,000 tax credit for any software-related programming or manufacturing job created in rural counties and also gave the company a 100 percent break on its state business and occupation tax.

Snyder, along with Senator Jim Hargrove of Hoquiam, also played a key role in persuading the state Department of Corrections to choose a 210-acre site southwest of Aberdeen as home to a new 1,936-bed prison. While many of Washington's small towns were vying for the prison, Snyder and Hargrove cornered Governor Lowry at an event and prodded him to push for the Grays Harbor site. The community itself mobilized to advance its case, steamrolling opponents. Some 600 jobs were created by the prison, Stafford Creek Corrections Center, which opened in 2000.

Mark Doumit, left, and Brian Hatfield, Snyder's former aide, were two members
of the influential Coastal Caucus. *Snyder family photo*

Snyder and Hargrove were two key longtime members of the nine-member Coastal Caucus, an informal, bipartisan alliance of lawmakers from both state houses geared toward advancing the interests of coastal Washington's 19th, 24th, and 35th legislative districts. Other prominent caucus members have included Lynn Kessler, Tim Sheldon, Mark Doumit, and Brian Hatfield, Snyder's protégé and former assistant. In recent years, Brian Blake, a former logger from Aberdeen, and Dean Takko, a former Cowlitz County assessor, have played key roles in the Coastal Caucus.

Kessler, a Hoquiam Democrat who eventually rose to House majority leader, said Snyder became a role model from the moment she declared her candidacy in 1992. "He was immediately warm, welcoming, and supportive, for which I was eternally grateful. I was struck by what a generous person he was." Once Kessler was elected and became a member of the powerful Coastal Caucus, she said she learned by observing Snyder. "He was the rudder; he was stability. If anybody was going off in some

Snyder stands behind President Bill Clinton during an event in 1994
in Seattle. *Snyder family photo*

As a senator, Snyder's door was always open. Here, in 1992, he stands outside it to greet crabber Ernie Summers of Westport. Kathy Quigg, *The Daily World*

counterproductive direction, he could always pull everybody back to where we really needed to be focused. He was always a gentle leader. He didn't lead with a brusque manner. He always led you there with a good conversation and a commonsense thought process, instead of telling us what to do. To watch Sid in action was a lesson in how to really get things done and how to conduct yourself in a way that's helpful, without a lot of crazy rhetoric. He was steady at the helm."

Despite his likability, Snyder took at least one noteworthy public hit during the mid-1990s. According to the *Seattle P-I*, in 1993-94 he accepted a number of gifts from influential interest groups, including Seafirst Bank, Boeing lobbyists, and the Western States Petroleum Association. When word of the story got to Snyder, he sent a letter to *The Daily News* of Longview stating he never again would accept gifts from lobbyists, even ones who were his friends. "The claims were asinine," the self-made millionaire said. "The way I saw it, is if someone invites you out to a dinner because they want to talk about something, you try to be polite and go. But am I going to sell my vote for a dinner? That's ridiculous."

Six months after he had his aortic valve replaced following a fainting episode, the 68-year-old Snyder fainted again, this time during an ad hoc legislative committee meeting in January 1995. Snyder slumped over in his chair and was immediately tended to by Senators Margarita Prentice, a registered nurse, and John Moyer, a physician. Snyder came to in less than a minute, but was wheeled into an ambulance that took him to St. Peter Hospital in Olympia. He had a pacemaker inserted the following morning, drove himself home to Long Beach at the end of the week, and was back at work in Olympia on Monday.

When Majority Leader Marc Gaspard resigned at the end of 1995 to lead the state's Higher Education Coordinating Board, Snyder was elected to succeed him. With a tenuous 25-24 majority in which party ranks often were broken, he had his hands full. If a Democratic member was sick, the best-laid plans could go awry. No longer was Snyder working the wheels behind the scenes. Now he was out front, acting as caucus spokesman, meeting with Republican leadership about bills that had been introduced, determining where they should be assigned, and making committee appointments. Snyder also was a board member of the important Economic and Revenue Forecast Council, which oversaw the preparation of, and approved, the state's official quarterly economic and revenue forecasts.

One major issue Majority Leader Snyder had to deal with early on was his caucus' support for Governor Lowry, which had dwindled to next to nothing. Sexual-harassment charges levied against the governor earlier that year by his former spokeswoman, Susanne Albright, had a lot to do with it. [Lowry agreed to pay her $97,500 out of his own pocket.] Further, nearly half the Senate Democrats had publicly pledged to back Nita Rinehart for governor the following year. Snyder did not endorse either Lowry or Rinehart, but many believed his head-to-head battle with the governor on a business-and-occupation tax-cut bill told them all they needed to know

Cruising in his car with Bette through Long Beach's Loyalty Day Parade was about all there was to Snyder's campaigning in 1996. By that time, he was so popular he did not need to campaign. He was unopposed that November. *Snyder family photo*

about whom he supported.

Compared with a year earlier, Snyder's health was in good shape in 1996, although some shocked Republicans maintained that his tongue could have used a tourniquet. In a January interview with a reporter from the *Seattle Post-Intelligencer*—Snyder believed the paper was out to do a "hatchet job" on him—he was asked what he thought of Linda Smith, the Republican firebrand recently elected to Congress from Southwest Washington. The day before the interview, Snyder had heard someone call Smith a "miserable bitch," so he used those words to describe her to the reporter, prefacing the description with "self-promoting" for extra emphasis. Snyder immediately realized he had slipped and asked the reporter not to print what he had said. She did anyway. Snyder's words created a mild uproar, although behind the scenes many praised him for saying precisely what they thought but never had the guts to say. One Democratic colleague, operating under the cloak of anonymity, told the *Seattle Weekly* two years later that Smith "is as self-centered a politician as you're ever going to meet. We all have ego. But she'll be at any place at any time to have her ego needs met."[5] Snyder agreed: "Most people didn't like Linda Smith. She was 150 percent for Linda Smith and that was it."

Snyder's dealings with Smith included an incident before the editorial board of *The Daily News* of Longview. Smith kept interrupting him. "We all got to say a few words and then were asked questions," Snyder said. "Linda had her say and I was trying to get my pitch out and she kept interrupting, kept interrupting. And I finally said, 'Excuse me, Linda, for talking while you're interrupting.' " *The Daily News* used Snyder's comment in the paper.

During the week that his "self-promoting miserable bitch" comment hit newsstands, Snyder asked for a point of personal privilege, rose on the Senate floor and issued a public apology to Smith. What he regretted was saying out loud what he really believed, but he did the gentlemanly thing.

Snyder won re-election unopposed in November, but lost his position as Senate majority leader because the Republicans had gained two seats to take a 26-23 majority. The Republicans also maintained strong control of the House. Although neither Rinehart nor Lowry ultimately decided to run, the Democrats retained the governorship. King County Executive Locke, a former legislator, easily defeated an arch-conservative Republican, Ellen Craswell, to become the country's first Chinese-American governor.

Nine ▪ A Whim and a Prayer

It turns out that Sid Snyder's headline-grabbing, seemingly spontaneous 1997 resignation was somewhat scripted. Snyder's tailspin, as he called it, had been conceived one day prior to his April 19 outburst on the Senate floor when he had learned that the majority Republicans had submitted a notice of reconsideration of a budget bill that was not eligible to be heard again without a two-thirds vote, which they could not muster. The Republicans' next step, and Snyder knew it was coming, was to pass a rule that allowed them to vote on the budget as many times as they wanted for the remainder of the session. Snyder believed it was legislative jujitsu to avoid amendments Democrats wanted.

Snyder told a couple of people, including Senate Democratic aide Marty Brown, what he was going to do if the Republicans followed through with their scheme. "It might seem kind of casual, but you're not talking about a Boy Scout meeting," Snyder recalled. "You're talking about running state government and a budget in the billions. They brought up the rule change and I walked out." Snyder's fellow Democrats followed him out of the chamber. Many Republicans were also shaken, including GOP counsel Milt Doumit, an Ilwaco native whose family had shopped in Snyder's grocery store since he was a child. "We tended to know what was happening around the Senate, but we had no idea it was coming," Doumit said. "You could hear the press guys say, 'Holy cow!' Everyone was rocked by it. It wasn't so much the political part—the process is the process, and it's not always pretty. For me, it was that an important role model was leaving. Sid was a legend."

Snyder and Republican Dan McDonald, the majority leader, discuss tax-cut legislation on the Senate floor at the end of January 1997, less than three months before the party leaders would square off on the budget-related rule change that led to Snyder's resignation. *Louie Balukoff*

Doumit, who went on to serve two years as secretary of the Senate, rose from his seat on the rostrum soon after Snyder walked past on his way out the door. Doumit left the floor, too. "I had built a relationship with him. I wouldn't have been able to contain my emotions if I had sat out there." He retreated to the journal clerk's office and sat alone, trying to soak in the enormity of what just had happened.

Snyder drove to Long Beach. The phone was ringing off the hook when he opened the door to his home, and it kept ringing for hours. He took some of the calls, including one from Gordy Walgren, who had tracked his progress from Olympia to the beach. "*What* are you doing?" the former majority leader admonished his old friend. Sid took Attorney General

Chris Gregoire's call, too. "I went apoplectic," Gregoire said. "I felt so close to him. 'Please don't do this,' I said. 'Please reconsider. You're the last person I would expect to do this.' He caught everybody off guard. He shocked us all. But it just took him over the edge. I couldn't imagine the loss of Sid at any time. We needed him at that point. We really did."

So affable did Snyder seem to most that his outburst surprised many of his colleagues, not to mention thousands of his constituents who saw the drama play out on television or those who read the stories beneath the next day's headlines. But Walgren had seen Sid mad before. So had others who were close to the senator. It was rare, they all said, but Snyder could get angry. "He did have a temper, but he used it very selectively," said Jeannine Roe, who served as Snyder's assistant for four years. "I can remember one occasion; it was a very justified chewing-out of a member who had betrayed him. He was yelling so hard that Vickie [Winters] and I were in the other room thinking, 'Please don't have a heart attack in there.' He really could let loose."

"He couldn't deal with lying and betrayal," added Winters, who worked for Snyder for six years. "If you're going to do something, just say you're going to do it. Don't lie and then go ahead and do it. That bothered him."

Snyder returned to Olympia with Bette the day after he quit to clean out his desk. Dan McDonald, the majority leader who had led the rule-changing effort that pushed Snyder over the edge, stopped by Snyder's office to express remorse over Snyder's departure and to explain why his party had done what it did. Snyder was touched. "I was crying. This was a big deal. As I sat there and talked to McDonald, I said, 'The rules in the Senate are more important than me. I've had a nice career. I'll go back to the grocery store.' That was it. I would be too embarrassed to come back. I would have lost any credibility that I might have."

Marty Brown was alerted by a security guard that Snyder was in his office packing. He took his 8-year-old son, who revered Snyder, to see him. The Browns helped the Snyders carry boxes to their car and waved as they watched the car drive away.

When the Senate honored the state champion Willapa Valley High School football team on the following Monday, the person who had drafted the resolution was not present. He was back in a grocery store that fronted a small-town main street, contemplating the events of the previous two days, lost in his thoughts amongst the meats and lingering malaise of having walked away from something that meant so much. Meanwhile, back in Olympia, the resignation letter he had told his assistant, Nyla Wood, to send to Governor Locke sat unsent on her desk. She knew her boss wanted to quit—and had heard him do so via a live audio feed piped into her office from the Senate floor—but she refused to allow it to happen. Nobody wanted Snyder to resign, not even the governor, who phoned asking him to reconsider: Take a few days off, Locke said. Cool down, and come back. Please.

The distance from Olympia to Long Beach provided Snyder with a 110-mile buffer, but he could not mentally separate himself from his other life. Had he been Joel Brown, Jehu Scudder, Henry Fiester, James Clark Strong or any of those other legislators of yesteryear, leaving Olympia would have been the end of it. But these were no longer territorial horse-and-buggy times. It was easy to get to Olympia now, and the phone calls kept coming. Big-city media came to him. After *The Seattle Times* sent a reporter to take the pulse of Long Beach, its headline read: "Resignation No Whim, Says Town that Knows Sen. Sid Snyder Best." Snyder had told the reporter, "I don't know what kind of circumstances could come about to cause me to go back."[1] The paper's editorial board also weighed in, saying Snyder had reason to be frustrated by "stubborn Republicans Pam Roach, Val Stevens and Bob McCaslin, who triggered the procedural crisis and forced their own leaders to throw out the rule book."[2] But the *Times* also was critical of the minority leader's move, calling it "… a sad and dramatic overreaction"[3] before conceding that "His resignation should sadden any citizen who longs for a more temperate and rational political climate."[4]

On Thursday, as Democrats and Republicans were spinning Snyder's resignation to suit their needs—and mailboxes in Long Beach and Olympia

The Daily World newspaper of Aberdeen was one of several media outlets to interview Snyder after he returned to office in April 1997. Kathy Quigg, *The Daily World*

were filling with laudatory letters—Snyder returned to Olympia. He was there to attend a reunion-style dinner with several former legislators and a few current ones. Senator Al Bauer, a Vancouver Democrat, handed Snyder a letter signed by every Democratic senator. They wanted him back. Senator Irv Newhouse, a Mabton Republican, was there, too. He had a similar letter of his own. It lacked a few of his colleagues' signatures but only because they had not been in caucus when it was drafted. Newhouse's letter read: "While we all recognize your objection to the procedural motion, we also realize that particular action cannot be undone at this point. But we hope your decision to resign is not yet final. There is good reason why we hope this is the case. The body needs individuals like you with your institutional history. Your legislative experience and knowledge are greatly missed. And your leadership will be valuable in the waning days of the session as we work on the important issues facing the citizens of this state."

The receipt of the letters marked the first time Snyder seriously considered returning. That Saturday, April 26, *The Daily News* in Longview ran a

Snyder works at his desk on the Senate floor with Republican floor leader
Irv Newhouse while Harriet Spanel waits to speak. *Louie Balukoff*

story saying Snyder was mulling a return. As the paper sat on newsstands, Snyder hopped in the car, Bette beside him, and headed back to Olympia. Along the way he called Bauer to tell him he was returning. He did not want fanfare, he told his friend. But Bauer could not keep a secret this big, not even for a couple of hours. When the Snyders pulled into the Capitol, reporters, photographers, and TV cameras were waiting.

Snyder had succumbed to lobbyists from the most powerful special-interest group he had ever known. When he returned to the Senate floor later in the day, that group—his colleagues—greeted him with a standing ovation. They had won him back with their respect. Dan McDonald did the official welcome-back duties: "It is awful good to have all 49 senators here. We are happy to have you back."[5] Snyder thanked McDonald and rose to his own personal privilege: "I'll tell you what happened: Bette's rules at home are tougher than the Senate rules, so I decided to go back. I'll do my best to behave most of the time."[6]

Snyder's return to the Capitol was not all rosy. He took some lumps for his about-face, particularly from the media. One newspaper, under the headline "Sid Snyder's sloppy decision to rejoin the Senate," wrote, "… for a few days there, he was a great legislator—before he lost sight of the goal and heeded to the chummy cry of the good ol' boys and agreed to rejoin a club of questionable virtue."[7] The Republicans also had taken at least one shot at Snyder during the week he was away: An amendment he had drafted to help the Sons of Norway Lodge in Cathlamet was jettisoned in the Senate before the bill it had been attached to was sent to Governor Locke.

The 105-day session closed the day after Snyder's return. He took advantage of the interim to have both hips, which had been bothering him for some time, replaced in separate surgeries. After the first, when the doctor informed Bette she would need to take care of her husband while

Snyder returned to the big office of Senate majority leader in 1999, after Democrats regained control. *Washington State Senate*

he recovered, she donned her Dr. Seuss hat and penned one of the Snyder family's all-time favorite poems:

> I did not want to be his nurse
> I sensed I'd only make him worse
> I did not want to dispense his pills
> I did not want to share his ills.
>
> I did not want to cook his meals
> The role of caregiver held no appeal
> I did not want to be calm and brave
> I'd even have to help him shave.[8]

By the end of the poem, the reluctant wife had caved—but she is punished for having done so.

> I persevered and Sid got well
> But I have this sorry tale to tell
> Said the doctor, "Bette I'm proud
> Of the courageous way you rallied 'round
> Now listen up—and get a grip
> I'll now replace his other hip!"[9]

After the second surgery, Snyder was driving again within three days and shortly thereafter attending meetings across his district. Whether Bette's aversion to taking care of him had anything to do with Sid's speedy recovery is hard to say. She is a persuasive woman.

By 1999, when Democrats were back in control of the Senate and Snyder once again was majority leader, any issues others may have had with him over his dramatic resignation and comeback had vanished. Snyder was back in the big office. It featured a framed Harry Truman poster, a small desk, and a glass-doored case full of legislative manuals dating back to statehood. He was earning $35,130 a year in Olympia, working each day from a calendar full of 30-minute appointments interrupted only by a couple of breaks scheduled in by aides who knew they—and Snyder—needed them. Those appointments frequently resembled half-hour sitcoms, with Snyder starring as the humorous grandfatherly lead. Marty Brown, who worked with Snyder in various capacities in the Senate beginning in the late 1970s, remembered that as the visitors departed Snyder's office they would say, "Wow, Sid just fixed the problem." And Brown would say, "Tell me what he did." Sid's secret, for all his fabled skills as a raconteur, was that "basically, he listened to them." That is what they all said. First, he would listen, Brown learned, "then he'd tell them a story that was kind of a metaphor. Then they'd leave, thinking their problem was fixed." Snyder, for all his life experience, surely was not an expert on each of the wide variety of concerns people brought to his office. But he was an expert on reading and relating to people. Crucially, he had been at the Capitol for 50 years—nearly half of Washington's statehood. He knew your predecessor, your boss, your father, your brother, your Uncle Bob. He was the bridge between old and new, a legislative historian in the truest sense because he had seen it all, or most of it, and he loved to talk about it. His stories about the sometimes bawdy adventures of Clyde V. "Tizzy" Tisdale, the legendary Pacific County legislator, were delivered with the skill of a gifted mimic—a cross between Mark Twain and Jay Leno.

On April 20, 1999, Snyder's colleagues from both sides of the Senate aisle chose to honor his golden anniversary at the Capitol with a surprise resolution. Hundreds were on hand, including friends, former colleagues, and family. Bette sat with her husband next to Lieutenant Governor Brad Owen at the top of the rostrum as the reading clerk intoned:

WHEREAS, A Senator by any other name cannot compare to our own Senator Sid Snyder, a man whose civility, credibility, respect for the legislative process and commitment to "do the right thing" remind us why we were elected to office; and …

WHEREAS, This master of Reed's Rules can bring a sweat to the brow of the opposition by simply thumbing through his "little red book" on the Senate floor; and …

WHEREAS, Back on the coast, trusting constituents have been known to hand over their ballots—as well as their grocery money—to the so-called "Governor of Southwest Washington"; and …

WHEREAS, Senator Snyder's distaste for skinny grocers has made him a self-proclaimed "light eater"—from daylight until dark; and

BE IT FURTHER RESOLVED, That the Senate thank his wife and family for sharing with the Legislature for the last fifty years the company and humor of this very decent and honorable man. [10]

After the reading, several senators shared memories. Harriet Spanel said she wished she had carried a tape recorder with her to record every conversation she had with Snyder to help preserve his stories for posterity. Dan McDonald told the story of posing in front of the sign at Snyder's market. Lorraine Wojahn praised Snyder's ability to keep decorum in the Senate. During the next 20 minutes, several others expressed similar sentiments, most tipping their cap to Bette as well. Sid fidgeted in the spotlight. Governor Locke came next: "You can take him at his word, and you can take his word to the bank."

When finally it was his turn to speak, Snyder choked back tears: "I have been privileged to be associated with this institution for 50 years. I don't think anybody could be as lucky as I have been. Probably the greatest blessing has been my family. It isn't always easy for families and spouses. It isn't easy when you miss baseball games or you miss the recitals or you miss

Snyder hugs longtime aide, Nyla Wood, during an April 1999 ceremony
honoring his 50 years at the Capitol. *Snyder family photo*

being home, day in and day out. Or in the evening when you are home
there's a meeting you need to go to and your spouse suffers."

Mike Flynn, publisher of the *Puget Sound Business Journal*, used the
occasion to sum up the essence of Sid: He was "viewed by his colleagues
on both sides of the aisle in the Legislature as the kind of lawmaker they'd
like to be, but know they can't be."[11] Later that year, retired senator Ray
Moore, who'd been both Republican and Democrat and never beat around
the bush, weighed in with his own tribute. In his own half-century in politics, Moore had known Dwight Eisenhower, Richard Nixon and Warren
Magnuson, to name a few, as well as hundreds of legislators. "To me," he
wrote, "one person is the ultimate standard by which I measure political
ability. He did it all while helping everyone with whom he worked, and
more importantly—without hurting anyone. Every politician could and
should learn from the best all-around politician in my memory. Had I
known Sid Snyder earlier, I might have been a better man."[12]

Snyder's 50th anniversary would have provided the perfect opportunity

Snyder proudly serves as an

Senate Majority Leader Sid Snyder and his wife, Bette, celebrated the Long Beach Democrat's 50-year career in the Legislature Tuesday, April 20 with the reading of an honorary Senate Resolution. Snyder, who began his Capitol career in 1949 as an elevator operator, was hailed by Gov. Gary Locke as "our legislative tribal elder." Hundreds of friends, family and colleagues gathered for the surprise event and reception that followed.

Senate Resolution
1999-8677

By Senators Spanel, B. Sheldon, Loveland, Bauer, Wojahn, McDonald, Stellar, Hale, Kline, Rasmussen, Heavey, Goings, Haugen, Fairley, Johnson, Patterson, Gardner, Eide, T. Sheldon, Long, Jacobsen, West, Zarelli, Rossi, Winsley, Deccio, Oke, Morton, McCaslin, Stevens, Franklin, Honeyford, Benton, Sheahan, Horn, Shin, Kohl-Welles, Thibaudeau, Hargrove and Costa

WHEREAS, In January 1949, a young man from Long Beach began his rise to Senatorial fame as an elevator operator in the State Capitol; and

WHEREAS, This same man has come to embody the institution he has served for the last fifty years, moving up from the Bill Room and the House of Representatives, to a nineteen year term as Secretary of the Senate, then to elected office as the State Senator from the Nineteenth District and finally to Senate Majority Leader; and

WHEREAS, A Senator by any other name cannot compare to our own Senator Sid Snyder, a man whose civility, credibility, respect for the legislative process and commitment to "do the right thing" remind us why we were elected to office; and

WHEREAS, His diplomacy as Secretary of the Senate and dedicated service to forty-nine bosses earned him the well-deserved title of "the Fiftieth Senator;" and

WHEREAS, While Senator Snyder may portray himself as a Democratic Donkey, he has the institutional memory of an elephant and the well-deserved title of Senate Historian; and

WHEREAS, This master of Reed's Rules can bring a sweat to the brow of the opposition by simply thumbing through his "little red book" on the Senate floor; and

WHEREAS, His personal charm and dedicated work ethic also proved valuable in his successful business endeavors, from Sid's Market to the Bank of the Pacific; and

WHEREAS, His passion for politics have often led his poetic "political widow" Bette Snyder and their three children, Sid Jr., Karen and Sally, "Home Alone" and running the store; and

WHEREAS, Back on the coast, trusting constituents have been known to hand over their ballots -- as well as their grocery money -- to the so-called "Governor of Southwest Washington";
and

WHEREAS, Senator Snyder's distaste for skinny grocers has made him a self-proclaimed "light eater" — from daylight until dark; and

WHEREAS, While in the majority, Senator Snyder has been known to run the Senate as he would a grocery store: volume, volume, volume;

and

WHEREAS
storytelling o
own mantra:
vote; when i
and

WHEREAS
gave new me
"wag the dog
beloved car
former Gover

WHEREAS
tener and wi

The Pacific County Press, April 28, 1999   Page 7

ected official for '50' years

Senate Majority Leader Sid Synder and his wife Bette.

nchant for
icts with his
he majority,
ority, talk;"

Snyder once
the phrase
e sat on the
panion of
Lee Ray;
a good lis-
ompromise,

Senator Snyder has earned the respect of both sides of the aisle; and
WHEREAS, His countless (and
often repeated) stories, imperson-
ations of Senator Clyde Tisdale and
sense of humor help keep us from
taking ourselves too seriously;
NOW, THEREFORE, BE IT RE-
SOLVED, That the Washington State
Senate congratulate and thank Senator Sid Snyder for his half-century
of dedicated public service, friendship and leadership; and

BE IT FURTHER RESOLVED,
That the Senate thank his wife and
family for sharing with the Legislature for the last fifty years the company and humor of this very decent
and honorable man.
I, Tony M. Cook, Secretary of the
Senate, do hereby certify that this is
a true and correct copy of Senate
Resolution 1999-8677, adopted by
the Senate April 20, 1999.

TONY M. COOK
Secretary of the Senate

for him to exit Olympia for good. His term was coming to a close; he was now in his mid-70s, and truth be told, he hated campaigning. "The most horrible job is raising money for campaigns," he said. "And then the treatment that you receive in the media and in talk shows. They just rip you apart. It's kind of disheartening." For all the talk about divisive politics, lawmakers would rarely rip you apart. "I've always said, in all the years I've been at the Capitol, I don't think there's any member that's served out there that I know that I wouldn't enjoy having as my next-door neighbor, regardless of the party they're affiliated with."[13]

Snyder considered not running for re-election in 2000, but finally decided he was not ready to let go. He had achieved his longtime, half-joking goal of living to see the 21st century, yet still had things he wanted to accomplish. It was not until July that he publicly announced he was going to run. Snyder easily fended off a challenge from Ron Mullins in the primary, and moved on to face Bill Schumacher, a retired Xerox engineer from Castle Rock. Schumacher was chair of the Cowlitz County Republicans, and he hit Snyder hard from start to finish. "The interests of our area have been sold out to extreme environmentalists and the liberal agenda of the Puget Sound Democrats," one press release declared. "It does no good to have a powerful senator from our area if he no longer represents the interests of the people in our area who elected him."[14] Come November, Snyder won 66 percent of the vote. He had raised $143,193 to his opponent's $15,920.

His powers at their peak, Snyder seemed to be everywhere at once. He helped stop an unpopular land swap on the Long Beach Peninsula that would have given 41 undeveloped acres of oceanfront property to a Vancouver developer in exchange for 48 acres of beachfront near Fort Canby State Park. He was instrumental in saving the Pacific Coast Cranberry Research Station from closure. He fought a U.S. Fish and Wildlife Service plan to relocate large numbers of salmon-eating Caspian terns from the Columbia River to Willapa Bay or Grays Harbor. He battled to pass a bill giving Pacific County residents a way to hold their own against what he saw as bullying by the Department of Ecology over pollution in Willapa Bay. He helped save the Naselle Youth Camp and its critical jobs and he secured $2.5 million for a major renovation at Station Camp, a spot near the mouth of the Columbia River where the Lewis and Clark expedition spent 10 days in November 1805. In August 2012, thanks to Snyder, his daughter Karen, the Chinook Indian Nation and dozens of others, the 280-acre Middle Village and Station Camp Park became part of the Lewis and Clark National Historical Park. He, along with the rest of the Coastal Caucus, also went head to head with Governor Locke over a 350-acre, Scottish links-style golf course being proposed at Half Moon Bay in Westport. "We were in a meeting with Governor Locke and a number of agency heads," said Lynn Kessler, House majority leader at the time. "The governor said all his agency heads said [the course] was a bad idea. Sid turned to the agency heads and said, 'So what is it you're afraid of?' And one of them said, 'We worry about jobs being lost.' Sid bristled: 'What are you talking about? This *is* about jobs!' He looked at the governor and said, 'What sense does this make, governor? Westport is almost dead from fishing decisions, clam viruses, environmental decisions.' He just challenged the governor. 'This is outrageous. They don't know anything about this community. Governor, I'm asking you right now to say that you will help us get this done.' And the governor looked at him and said, 'I'll help you.'"

Statewide, Snyder pushed for transportation taxes he felt would boost commerce by improving Washington's gridlocked roads, and supported legislation to help build a second bridge across the Tacoma Narrows. He rolled his eyes as Mukilteo's anti-tax crusader, Tim Eyman, pitched initiatives to handcuff the Legislature by requiring two-thirds votes on tax measures. As lawmakers' expenses rose in the midst of a recession, Snyder covered more of his costs out of his own pocket. A *Seattle Post-Intelligencer* study conducted in 2001 found Snyder ranked 44th of 49 senators in spending.

The third major earthquake to hit Western Washington during Snyder's half-century with the Legislature struck shortly before 11 a.m. on February 28, 2001. This time, Snyder was at the Capitol—one of the scariest locations of all—as the 6.8-magnitude quake rippled up from the tectonic plates far below. He was in the caucus room at the south end of the Senate chamber on the third floor of the stately 73-year-old Legislative Building. The lawmakers, pages, aides and hundreds of others from the Capitol's offices fled through the marbled halls as the massive chandelier in the great domed rotunda swayed. Standing outside, Snyder said, "we tried to use our cellphones but most of them were plugged because there were so many calls going through."

That Snyder's version of the story, filtered by his humility, ends there says more about the man than were he to add a thousand more words, or even a hundred thousand, to his picture of what unfolded on the lawn. Fortunately, others were there, including his legislative assistant, Vickie Winters, so we know the rest of the story, one that speaks volumes about Snyder's sense of decorum. After everyone else had safely left the building, Winters recalled, Snyder came out, rule book in hand, and huddled with the crowd of evacuees near the southeast door of the Legislative Building. There, he and Lieutenant Governor Brad Owen officially declared the end of the day's session. Winters was touched. "When most of us were stunned and staring, Sid had the presence of mind and such reverence for the in-stitution that he made certain the Senate rules were observed and that the session was properly adjourned. It was a powerful example of this amazing statesman's calm, steady ability to think clearly and lead through crisis."

Former Senator Mark Doumit also fondly recalled the reverence Snyder had for the Capitol. "One time after a late-night budget meeting Sid and I were walking through the Capitol and he just stopped. He reached up and put his hand on a marbled column in the Legislative Building and he looked at me and commented, 'What an awesome opportunity for a couple of guys like us from small towns to be here doing this work.' "

Snyder also occasionally stepped on his tongue. A week after the terror-ist attack of September 11, 2001, he and state Revenue Director Fred Kiga were sitting next to each other during a public meeting of the Revenue Forecast Council. Snyder compared the event to the Japanese surprise attack on Pearl Harbor. "One thing I do want to warn, though, is that, as we said in those days, the common theme was, 'Well, we'll take care of those Japs in six weeks.' Well, we know it lasted four years."[15] Snyder immediately realized his faux pas. Although "Japs" had been ubiquitous when he was growing up during World War II, it now was considered highly derogatory, particularly to Kiga, a Japanese-American. Snyder quickly realized his mistake and apologized. "I felt horrible," he said. Kiga accepted Snyder's apology.

Snyder's battle with prostate cancer made newspaper headlines during the 2002 session, but hardly affected the man himself. "I'm not worried or concerned," he told one reporter. "The doctor even said one option would be to do nothing, that it would take so long to get me that something else would take me first."[16] Snyder had radiation treatments. Follow-up tests showed he was cancer-free. By July, he was feeling fine, and he and his family flew to Denver for the annual meeting of the National Conference of State Legislatures. There, Snyder received what he considered to be one of his greatest honors, the prestigious Excellence in State Legislative Leadership Award. The award is bestowed each year upon a state legislative leader whose "career embodies the highest principles of leadership—integrity, compassion, vision and courage." Snyder was awarded $10,000 to donate to a cause of his choosing. He split the money between Lower Columbia College in Longview and Grays Harbor College in Aberdeen. He said it would not have been fair for him to choose one of his district's schools over the other. Snyder also gave $10,000 of his own money to help launch the Ilwaco branch of Grays Harbor College, and later, along with his friend Pat Dunn, purchased two wooden "Welcome to Ilwaco" signs. One was installed at the north entrance to town, the other at the south entrance. Neither man ever asked for credit. Snyder said they did it because they "felt the struggling town deserved something special." For the same reason, he sponsored a student-essay contest at his alma mater, Kelso High. A total of $1,000 is awarded each year, $500 to the winner, all from Snyder's pocket.

As voters gathered at the polls on November 5, 2002, to pass judgment on $30 car tabs, house resolutions, legislative hopefuls and old hands, Snyder sent out a press release: "It's time for me to be with my wife, Bette. Her unwavering support of me and my career has been a big part of any successes I have achieved. Now, I need to be with her more than I need to serve in the Senate." Snyder had chosen Election Day to ensure that day's results had no effect on his decision or anyone's interpretation of it. He was retiring to be with Bette.

A Democratic scramble ensued. No one could replace him, but who would be appointed to succeed him? Snyder struggled to not concern himself with such matters. His was not a political decision. It was a human one. Bette had fallen at home and broken a few ribs. A detached retina had led to eight surgeries, and eventually the loss of her right eye. *Bette needed him more.*

Snyder cleaned out his desk, again; loaded his car, again. He pulled from his wallet a tattered copy of a prayer once used to open a Senate session, and read it to himself:

> Our Heavenly Father, we are grateful for the excellent rating our legislators have earned through the years. Bless them in their work today. Give them a pride of office and a workmanship that is sensitive to popular opinion but refuses to be enslaved by it. Let them be men of courage, preserving the best of the past, yet boldly creative in those areas where past solutions no longer serve present needs. And deliver them from the harassment of all Monday-morning quarterbacks, who having never played the game, still regard themselves of All-American caliber. Amen.

This time, Snyder was *really* not going back. And he rarely did. "If you break up with your girlfriend," he said, "you don't hang out at her house."

There was no mistaking what led to Snyder's final retirement in 2002.
It was so he could spend more time with Bette. *Snyder family photo*

In 2008, the City of Kelso dedicated a bench outside City Hall to Snyder.
Snyder family photo

Ten ▪ Sine Die

Forever ago begins in the Legislative Building at the end of Sid Snyder Avenue in Olympia. Memorabilia-filled boxes are tucked under office desks and crammed into storage closets; official portraits hang on walls, and stories move from mouths to minds. They are told by those who knew Sid Snyder way back when, as well as those who know him only through legend.

Forever ago ends in Kelso, down the road from a shiny metal-and-wood bench honoring a native son. The bench is outside City Hall, the first building on the Kelso side of the Allen Street Bridge, where South Pacific Avenue begins its two-lane trek down the Cowlitz River to the Stop 'n' Shop, the store where Sally McNulty has worked—even lived—for the past three decades. She can tell you how much cheaper it is to buy beer at her place than the golf course across the way. She can tell you the history of her small store, how it once was fronted by a dirt road that flooded so badly that residents had to tow their farm animals to the hilltops to keep them from drowning. She can tell you her place once was owned by a couple named Kreiger. And if you stay long enough, she will tell you about the special boy that couple hired—the 12-year-old who walked to work from a nearby home that is long gone. Yet, oddly, the utility pole that once powered the home still stands. Tattooed through its midsection by rusted nails supporting the metal numbers "1405," the pole is flanked by a grimy motor home, three vehicles topped with tarps, and a neighborhood of houses that have seen better days. It storms a lot here.

Retirement took place on the Long Beach Peninsula, five miles north of The Bank of the Pacific on Sid Snyder Drive, and six miles north of Sid's Market, which had been passed on to a son who, conveniently, has the same name as the legendary man who founded it a half-century earlier. Sid and Bette Snyder's days together were spent in a 4,000-square-foot beachfront home built for a retirement that came, went, and then came again. The elevator and wide doors were concessions to advancing age and its inevitable assorted ailments. The downstairs office closely resembled one that, forever ago, existed on the third floor of the Capitol. Its walls and small tables were filled with photos of the occupant posing with governors and presidents, and decades worth of awards. The Robert F. Utter Award, given in 2008 by the Washington State YMCA's Youth & Government board for a history of civic leadership and being an outstanding role model for teens, was one. The C. David Gordon Award, given in 2010 by the Association of Washington Business, was another. Red-covered legislative manuals sat atop the desk, as did a bronze nameplate that once existed in an office on the third floor of the Capitol.

Upstairs, the phone still rang. Former constituents sought assistance with predicaments. Former colleagues sought advice on procedures. Old friends wanted to shoot the breeze with someone they missed. Former Governor Gary Locke called from China to chat. Governor Chris Gregoire called to say he was missed. She needed his advice, too. Her fondness for Sid Snyder—the person and the legislator—was unmistakable. She believed the country would be far better off if there were several Sid Snyders in Congress. "Sid wouldn't let ideologue or partisanship get in the way," she said. "He's a man who understands the institution and how it works at its best. He will go to bat for the institution. When he was in office, he was considered in the highest regard. He left office and he's still considered the same."

Mariners games pulled the Snyders north to their Seattle condominium. They had done so every year for decades, but in later years it had taken a big game or special occasion, such as the time in September 2012 when Bette threw out the first pitch after she and Sid were honored as the organization's Fans of the Year. To have seen Bette Snyder pantomime "YMCA" with the gusto of a teenager during the seventh-inning stretch is to have seen a wondrous sight. To have seen Sid shake his head and ask a friend, "Can you believe she's 89?" was, too.

But most retirement days were quiet in the Snyder home. When there was talk, it was more often about the recent doings of grandkids—Melissa, Calvin, Whitney, and Cole—than of any tales of past accomplishments or late-night drama at the Capitol. Two topics al-

A lifelong baseball fan, Snyder was honored by the Seattle Mariners in 2006 with the chance to throw out the first pitch. *Snyder family photo*

ways brought Snyder to tears: The 61 years he and Bette were married and the stroke Sid Jr. suffered in his 50s that derailed a stellar law career but also brought him back to town to carry on the legacy of the family market—and to carry on the tradition of handing out discontinued Kennedy half-dollars as change to customers, because Dad dearly loved the coins and the president they represented. Snyder sometimes talked of regrets, like not keeping a daily journal, then wondered who would want to read it. "People will have forgotten who Sid Snyder is after a few years," he said,

Snyder hands Sid Jr. the keys to Sid's Market. "We didn't even need to change the name of the store," Snyder laughed. *Snyder family photo*

One year after Snyder's retirement, the City of Long Beach renamed 10th Avenue Southwest after him. *Snyder family photo*

Snyder's family returned to Olympia in 2006 for a ceremony to rename the road leading into the Capitol after him. *Washington State Senate*

"but I had dreams. I was never afraid of work, and no job was below me. I think that people who know me, have been acquainted with me, have dealt with me on a personal basis, or a legislative basis, or a neighborly basis, I hope they say that I was fair. I think that would be more important than anything. But probably the biggest legacy that I'll leave is, 'Who is this Sid Snyder guy that they named the street after?'"

Streets. **Sometimes they slice across peninsulas** until their pavement is overtaken by sand and saltwater. Sometimes they cut through well-manicured lawns, where squirrels scamper in the spring, until they bump into big buildings where debates can become contentious and bills become law. Sometimes they are named after giants or gentlemen. Sometimes one name can symbolize both.

Sid Snyder Oral History

THIS IS AN EDITED COMPILATION of oral history interviews conducted by Sharon A. Boswell, John C. Hughes, and Jeff Burlingame, beginning in 2006 and continuing up to just weeks before Snyder's death. Transcription by Pat Durham and Lori Larson.

Your story, to me, seems to be the American Dream. The way you started out in the Depression. Did you ever dream that you would ...

No, no, no. I know I've come to as close to living the American Dream as anybody.

Tell me how that dream got started.

I was born in Kelso on July 30, 1926, when my dad was 57 and my mother was 43. My dad, Alfonso Snyder, was 62 when he died. They called him "Fonny." He spent 31 years in the Eighteen-hundreds and he spent 31 years in the Nineteen-hundreds. He died when I was five, so I really don't have any memories of my father to speak of. My dad was a barber, and I know very little about him even though I had three older brothers. We never seemed to ever talk much about my dad.

What else do you know about your dad?

I have some addresses where he barbered, or where he lived. I don't know very much about my father's side of the family. One of our daughters has tried to contact people, and has never been very successful in finding out much about him. My mother's side we know quite a bit about. My grandmother, Caroline McBee, walked across the Plains from Missouri in 1852 in a wagon train. Her mother and father, Levi and Elizabeth McBee, both died along the way. My grandmother was 10 when she arrived in Portland in the fall of 1852. She worked around—as a domestic—until she was 14. She married at 14 in Roseburg, Oregon, to a fellow by the name of Rufus Horatio Beeman. My grandparents were married just a couple of weeks short of 68 years. Back in those days that was quite a feat. They had 14 children. My mother was the 13th. My grandfather died a couple of years before I was born. After Roseburg, they moved over into what is now called Columbia County. I think it originally was all part of Walla Walla County during the days when Washington was part of the Oregon Territory. I had aunts and uncles who were born in the 1860s or late 1850s, in that area. And then they moved over into the Nez Perce country. I'm sure my grandfather knew Chief Joseph.

What were they doing for work?

They were farmers. And then they moved up into the Okanogan coun-try. I have a book we call *The Beeman Book* that a cousin of ours wrote in the early '70s. She traced the Beeman family tree. It goes back to a Thomas Beeman, who died at age 74 in Kent, Connecticut, in 1750. His mother-in-law was born in Salem, Massachusetts, in 1644, I believe.

I'd love to see that book.

I'll get it out for you. There are a lot of interesting stories in there. If we go back to the mother-in-law, I think I'm the eighth or ninth generation in this country, which is kind of unbelievable. One of the Beeman women was married to Brigham Young and they had two sets of twins that died as infants. I had three older brothers. One time, my grandmother was visiting when I was about two-years-old and my second-oldest brother, Vic, needed a paper for school. He was in typing class—I think the only boy who took typing in those years—which would have been about 1928. He typed up a story about my grandmother talking about coming across the Plains.

Do you still have it?

Yes. And it's part of *The Beeman Book*. It kind of ends when she gets married, but there are other stories to back it up. There's a page out of a history book on North Idaho that was printed probably about the turn of the century. My grandfather is in there. He ran for sheriff of Nez Perce County and lost by one vote back in the 1880s. My mother was born in 1883. I think it was about then that he was in the grocery business. I think it said their business was good, but collections were poor and he was forced to retire from the business. This story about my grandmother coming across the Plains is in there. In the Sunday section of the Spokane paper in about 1950, there's an article about a couple of the Beeman boys and their early exploits. There's a story about my grandfather in the Nez Perce country. They raised all these hogs and had all this bacon and there was no market for it. He took it up to Canada and sold it to the Canadians in the Okanogan country. There were no roads. There were no trails. They had to make their own. They had to ford rivers. They had grease made out of the bacon. I think they got 25 cents a pound for the bacon, which was pretty good in those days.

Was growing up without a father difficult for you, emotionally or as a practical matter?

I don't think so. My mother was a great mother. She could stretch a dollar. We lived in South Kelso. We had a big garden. I raised rabbits and sold them around. We had our own chickens, and canned fruit, and made applesauce from the Gravenstein apple tree in the backyard. My mother took in washing, mainly from teachers that were bachelors. I don't know what she got—probably 10 cents a shirt, and I got a few tips when I delivered them.

How much was a rabbit going for?

Under a dollar, I'm sure.

Tell me more about your mother.

She lived to be 94. When we got into World War II, jobs became plentiful and she went to work in the shipyards. She was about 60-years-old and she was crippled with arthritis. In later years, she had to get around with a crutch and a cane. But she never complained, never at all, about her lot in life. She had a good sense of humor and she was always proud of her kids and what they accomplished.

Obviously, she instilled a strong work ethic.

Absolutely. Of course we didn't know anything else.

How much older were your brothers?

My oldest brother graduated from high school in 1926, the year I was born. In 1908, my brother Floyd was born, and December of 1910 my brother Vic was born. My brother Rufus was born in 1921.

With such an age gap, were any of the brothers close?

I think the older two were kind of close, but there was quite a bit of spread.

Were they good to their kid brother? Were they guys you looked up to or were you pretty much on your own?

Pretty much on my own. Another thing about my brother Vic. He got pneumonia as a baby, and the doctors said they didn't think he was going to make it. But my mother pulled him through with all the old mustard poultices and other home remedies. It left him with weak lungs all his life. The other three of us were all in the service during World War II, but they wouldn't take Vic. In later years when he'd come to visit with us he'd walk up the five or six stairs and he'd just be wheezing. I'll tell you a story that's hard to believe now: About the time he was a senior in high school or a little later, he went to the doctor about his lungs and his difficulty breathing. The doctor was the leading doctor in Longview at the time, and he recommended he take up smoking. He thought it would be good for his lungs to breathe in and out. He died from emphysema. I think he was about 74.

What did you want to be when you grew up?

I wanted to be in business of some kind.

Well, you were running a business with your wagon. Selling rabbits and delivering laundry.

And we sold vegetables out of our garden. I'd drag it around and sell the vegetables. I don't know what we made from them, but not a lot.

You're the natural-born business man, from the crucible of the Depression like millions of other people who grew up with hardship. What was that like?

We didn't know we were in a Depression. It was just the way it was.

I know you had various jobs growing up at Kelso. Tell me about stacking the dry kiln at the mill.

Did it by hand. Lumber came in and it went through a drop-sorter. You worked in pairs. Your partner would start to pull the lumber off where the drop-sorter left it. You started with just wheels on a track and you put the first level down and then you put a sticker between each layer as you went up. The stacks—two-by-fours, or whatever it was—ended up about 10 feet high.

How much did that pay?

About 95 cents an hour. It was piece work. The more you did the more you got paid. So I would make up to $12 a night. That, I thought, was probably the most money I'd ever make in my life. You had a leather apron on, and leather gloves, and leather whatever it was that covered your whole arms. Otherwise you'd be all splinters.

It seems you were incredibly driven.

I've never been afraid of work, that's for sure. A lot of times I've had two jobs.

Where were you when you heard about Pearl Harbor, Sid? When you think back can you just vividly remember hearing Roosevelt's voice, and what that was like?

Oh, yeah.

Getting philosophical on you, but what were your thoughts on war? Specifically World War II, but war in general?

Didn't Roosevelt also say, "I hate *waaaar*"? He had that patrician accent. I think there were a few conscientious objectors around, but most of us were patriotic. There was no question about it.

Were you afraid of potentially going into battle?

No. We had a song we sang: "They promised me wings of silver. They promised me bars of gold. They made me an aerial gunner. I'll die when I'm 18 years old."

Were there any Japanese Americans around Kelso when you were growing up?

Yes. I remember a family, the Myedas, who were from Longview. They were detainees. They had a laundry. There were three sons. One of them fought in Italy with the U.S. Army and one of them was killed. After the war, the two boys took over the laundry. So many Japanese people lost their businesses or farms. I couldn't tell you how they got through it without losing their faith. Roosevelt put out that order to detain the Japanese, and we didn't like it, I remember that, because of the people we knew. I guess on the other hand, most just thought the president was doing the right thing, and didn't think that people's rights were being violated like they were. My brother Rufus, in later years, worked as a laundry driver for the Myedas. I knew them quite well. In fact, one of the boys was in my brother's class. He graduated in 1940 from high school. They came to Long Beach quite often.

You were interested in the Army Air Force. Why?

Two of my brothers were in it. It intrigued me, I guess. I wasn't particularly fond of being in the Navy because I tend to get seasick.

I'm curious to know your first political stirrings?

Everybody was a Democrat in my neighborhood except for one classmate, Bob Berry, who everybody called "senator." He was the only Republican around. When he died, his obit in the Longview *Daily News* went from the top of the page, one column, to the bottom. He ended up being a little bit of everything. He was in the military. He was a lieutenant colonel. He was in the Pentagon. He just did all kinds of things.

Did you fellows remain friends over the years?

Oh yeah, in fact at our last class reunion we did the program together.

Were you and Bob among the most successful members of Kelso High School's Class of 1944? Did you have a nuclear scientist?

No. But we had successful people, but I never thought about it like that. But Bob Berry was quite a guy.

What did it say in your high school annual? Was there anything predicting what you were going to grow up to be?

No. There's something in there, but it wasn't that.

But Bob Berry, he was a Willkie kind of guy and everybody else was for FDR?

Yep. We all called him "senator," but probably none of us thought I'd ever grow up to be the senator.

Retaining your friendship with him might have been one of the first examples of you working across the aisle.

Could be, yeah. By the way. I was always called "Bob." My full name is Sidney Robert Snyder.

Growing up you were "Bob?" When did that change?

Probably about the time I went to work down in Longview because they'd always take first name, middle initial. And going into the service it was the same thing. I think another reason it got changed to "Sid" was every time you said "Bob" about half the people in the class turned their heads. One of my older brothers had a high school teacher named S. Robert—can't think of his last name now. So my brother thought S. Robert was what my name should be.

But until you were about 14 or 15 everyone knew you as Bob?

Oh, yeah. I was Bob for a while down here in Long Beach, too. Bob and Bobby both. My mother finally took to calling me Sid, but it was kind of a struggle for her.

How about your brothers? Did they continue calling you Bob forever?

Not forever. But years later I remember being in the Long Beach Peninsula Loyalty Day Parade and some people I grew up with in South Kelso would shout, "Hey, Bobby!"

When you first met Bette Kennedy in 1950 were you Sid or Bob?

I was Sid.

What was Long Beach like when you first moved there in 1946?

It was a lot different. When Labor Day came, the tourists were gone. We had a theater, though. On Monday, Labor Day night, when the movie was out, people would go into a little ice cream parlor and then head home. There were two or three cars on the street and that was it. If you saw any tourists around in the wintertime, you looked at them a little strangely. Most of the motels closed up. It used to be that my store was even closed on Christmas and Thanksgiving. We're open on Christmas and Thanksgiving now. There's a crowd of out-of-town people who come over Thanksgiving Day and are around for that weekend. Christmas and New Year's there's a crowd of people. So it was a tourist town way back then, but it's changed a lot.

So it's more year-round tourism than it ever was before?

Yes. Even though there are not that many people around on weekdays.

The permanent population, what did they do for a living? There was still some logging and other things around, right?

Yes, logging. There were cranberries, oysters, fishing out of Ilwaco, and commercial fishing and sport fishing.

In 1949, you met one of your mentors, Si Holcomb. Tell me about him.

Si was born over in Ritzville. Wheat country. He had worked at the Capitol for years. The Republicans had control until 1932 and the Roosevelt landslide. The House of Representatives went from eight Democrats to 71. There was a fellow by the name of Ole Olsen from Pasco. He was a newspaperman. He was one of the eight Democrats that had been in the House in 1931, but he decided to run for lieutenant governor, and he got beat in the primary by Vic Meyers. So they chose Olsen to be the chief clerk. And when the regular session was over in '32, Governor Martin named him the state printer. Si Holcomb, who I worked for for years, became chief clerk in the special session of 1933. That's the year that they had a special session for the Steele Act that set up the liquor laws in the state.

That just got changed recently.

Yes. Sid's market now sells liquor. So Si was chief clerk. In 1947, the Republicans regained control of the House. But they kept him on—unheard of. Then they lost again and Si still kept his job. In 1953, however, when the Republicans gained control again, they replaced him. In 1955, the Democrats regained control, 50-49. So Si came back. And he was chief clerk until he died in 1965. Here's another little story: There were two brothers from Ilwaco, Jack and Reese Williams, who had been in college with Si. The three of them joined the ambulance corps in World War I, all of them together.

All of them?

Yes. It's funny how things are sometimes timed together.

Although assistant chief clerk was a partisan job, the Republicans kept Si on. That's pretty impressive.

They just didn't have anybody else. Years later, they kept me on when Pete von Reichbauer switched parties in '81, tilting control of the Senate to the Republicans. In fact it was the first time in 28 years that Republicans had achieved control of both chambers of the Legislature and the governor's office. They kept me partly because they didn't have anybody really for the job. And I hadn't mistreated them.

That 1981 session was a crazy one.

Yes it was. Revenues were way down. The shortfall was a billion dollars. They had two special sessions. They'd raised taxes a little bit and cut the budget a little bit, but they should have done it all at once. Most of the Republicans would admit that afterwards. We should have come in and just raised the sales tax a full penny instead. I kind of compare it with a youngster who has a new puppy and he has to cut the tail off. So he cuts it off a half inch at a time so it wouldn't hurt as much. That's what happened. But the Republicans had cut so many times that it really hurt them when they got back in the next election.

I heard a wonderful story. Somebody told me that after von Reichbauer jumped ship, a Republican leader came back a few months later and told the Democratic leadership, "You can have him back." Because he was such a mercurial guy.

Yeah. And it was a horrible session. You go back in the *Journal* and look. We were in session I'd say 100 hours out of the 168 hours in a week. The members went home to get some sleep, but the workroom crew stayed to get ready for the next day. I should never have allowed it, looking back, but some of the people went home, took a shower, changed clothes and came back. If you did it today, you know, everybody's all over you. But we tried to get done in 105 days, and didn't quite make it. They took a couple days off and they came back for a day to finish up the session. They had to come back for another 24 days later in the year because the revenue shortfalls just kept on coming. By the way, Peter, I've been told, is "the councilman from Arizona."

Regarding his role on the King County Council?

Yeah, he leaves every week and goes to Arizona, flies back and has his staff take care of things.

He must have a good staff.

Yeah. Must have.

Let's go back to 1949 when you starting working at the Capitol as an elevator operator. Sessions were 60 days then, every other year. What did Si Holcomb do in the interim?

I think he lived by his wits a little bit, and he had connections. One thing I can remember was that he would find good locations for service stations. I don't know if that was through his connections as chief clerk and he was doing it for the oil lobbyist's industry or whatever it was. He had an office in Seattle. And Si, like I say, was chief clerk when it didn't pay much. He strung it out as much as possible. He and John O'Brien, who was speaker of the House for four sessions, didn't get along very well be-cause one of the things Si did, which I didn't know for a long time, was he sold services to lobbyists.

Had you known that what would you have thought about it?

Well, I certainly didn't approve of it. I wouldn't have done anything like that.

Would knowing about it have been enough for you to walk away?

I doubt it because that was his deal. I wasn't getting any kickbacks from anybody. In fact, for years when I was in the Senate I used to give back part of my salary. Never made it public. I didn't do it for the publicity. I did it because I thought it was the right thing to do when the state was having tough financial times.

How did that work?

I would have liked it if they had just reduced my salary, but you can't do that. You've got to take your salary. So I had to give it back as a donation to the state. I used to give back $500 a payday, $1,000 a month.

So you just took your check, cashed it, and sent them a separate check?

No. It would just show as a deduction.

Si may have had his hang-ups, but he did teach you a lot, didn't he?

He taught me parliamentary procedure. They don't pay any attention to it anymore. It's a forgotten art, but it used to be that you did everything by the rule book—even the smallest detail. The rules say that you can't make a speech and then make a motion. They do that all the time now. Years ago, if you got up and made a speech and then moved to refer the bill back to Rules or something, five people would have been on their feet, "Point of order, Mr. Speaker. The motion's out of order!" It's really gone to pot, I think. Ask someone like Don Brazier, who wrote a history of the Legislature. Don Brazier will tell you that when Jim West left and I left, everything changed. No one is paying any attention to the rules. It's pathetic.

Is it because there aren't people like Si and Sid who are enforcing the rules?

It was part of the decorum. Sometimes you'd get tied up for two or three hours on parliamentary maneuvering. You'd go back and look up rulings from years ago and there was a precedence that had been set. There were books on those. It was just the way you did business, and I think the proper way.

What was the strength of that? Why have such a strict system?

I think one reason is that rules are made to protect the minority yet give the power and authority to the majority, so the minority can't block things forever. I think it allows for better discussion of the issues. They used to have real debates. Now they roll the budget out, two people make speeches on each side of it and then there's roll call. It used to be three or four hours and lots of amendments and lots of good, healthy debate on those amendments. That's all lost now. It's just more like Boy Scout camp where everything rolls along. Oh, sure, sometimes somebody raises a point of order.

Has it changed because people just don't learn parliamentary procedure?

I don't think they learn and they don't realize the importance. And there's so much to do in so little time. They think parliamentary procedure is a hindrance to rushing things through. The worst thing that happened is the automatic roll call machines. Look at how fast they turn those bills out. Not that they're not discussed in caucus and in committee. They get a pretty thorough going over, but they still bang them out: *Wham. Wham. Wham.* In the Senate they call the roll and it gives you time to talk with somebody about what's up next or what's up two or three items down the calendar.

The Senate has made a point of preserving that system, the roll call?

Yes. So far. I don't know if they'll always do that. They turn out some of those bills in the House on those consent calendars so quickly it's ridiculous because they don't know what they've voted for. I'm not saying that you always knew what you voted for in the Senate, but you had a pretty good idea. You'd get a little time to talk and sometimes hold bills. I don't think they hold bills on the calendar as much as they used to. And it was different, too. You went right down the calendar. The Rules Committee meant something. You got a bill out on the calendar, and you took it in that order. You didn't have that side list where you wonder what you are going to take up next. You would hold bills down the calendar. Somebody may have wanted to prepare an amendment or somebody didn't think they had the votes for the bill. The Rules Committee doesn't mean a thing now.

Is that also partially because you don't have a person with that institutional memory in place, like a Si Holcomb or yourself?

I think so. Yes. The importance of it is stressed less as we go along.

What were your duties in the bill room when you were promoted from the elevator in 1949?

The bill room was located right off of the House floor where the majority leader's office is now. It's very similar to the joint bill room. But you didn't have all the modern conveniences that you have today. The bills went down to the printer. You had the original bill and you had five mimeographed copies. So whoever was typing those, if they made a mistake, they had to go through six copies to correct it. Then you sent the corrected bills down to the printer and the Linotype operator would set them for the printing press. Well, the Linotype operator's version wouldn't be the same as the original bill, so that called for more corrections. One went to the printer and one went to the person who did the bill digest, and so forth. When you got the bill back from the printer, you put those in the bill books—that's what we did. The bill books were laced together, so you pulled them apart to add the new bills. If you amended one of those bills, you would say, "Page 3, line 8 of the original bill being page 4, line 6 of the printed bill." So you can see how much more cumbersome things were. There were evening sessions a lot of times, and then you did your work afterwards. I can remember lots of nights we'd work half the bill room until 12 or one o'clock in the morning and send them home, and then the rest of the crew would work until the work was done. Maybe the people you'd sent home at one o'clock in the morning would come back at eight, and the people who had been there all night long were still there. This didn't happen all the time, but it happened frequently.

Did being in the bill room give you a good perspective of the whole legislative process?

I think so, yes. You saw how things worked.

Not only were you right there, but you also were seeing all the bills and all their forms and whatever. Was it easy for errors to creep in?

There were errors, but I can't remember anything that was so gross that you couldn't change it in the next session. They change everything in the next session. They do find errors now, such as where the same section of the code gets amended twice and the changes aren't made correctly. There's less of that now because of the computers. It's so easy to make those changes. But, yes, there was probably more of that in those days. There were a lot of bills introduced, but not as many as today. You didn't have the cutoffs like we have today. The only cutoffs were the ones in the Constitution. It says in there that in the regular session you can't introduce a bill after the 40th day.

Was the pace much more intense because you only had a 60-day session every other year?

I think it was, even though it's also very intense now because they try to do so much in such a short length of time. And society is much more complicated.

When you went into the bill room, was it Si Holcomb, your boss, who had the oversight and would show you what to do? He kind of mentored you?

I kind of learned what to do in that one session. I didn't really need a lot of help, because it wasn't really rocket science. It was just a lot of hours. A lot of hard work.

And a willingness to do the hard work.

Yes.

You were talking about being wide-eyed coming into the Legislature for the first time. During that first session in '49, did you get to interact with Governor Art Langlie, a Republican?

Not really. But I met Al Rosellini, who was in the Senate. He was in the wings of the House one day and we all thought, "There's a pretty important guy." We all knew that at the time.

What about working with Charlie Hodde?

Charlie was speaker in '49.

Tell me a little bit about him.

I remember in '51—I was still in the bill room then—I went to work probably a week or so early and Charlie came over that week from his place. There wasn't any Committee on Committees. And I remember some members being around and Charlie came walking in. They asked, "What committees am I on?" Charlie reached in his coat pocket…

Standing from left, Bob Charette, Snyder, and Bob Bailey watch as Governor Al Rosellini signs a piece of legislation in 1963. *Washington State Legislature*

He had his whole list of who was where?

Yes. Charlie had sat down at home and he did it all. Charlie was a good speaker and a good guy. I enjoyed him.

He, obviously, was a real hands-on speaker.

Yes. There was a bill banning firecrackers up for consideration when Charlie was speaker. A fellow who sat in the front row was a Native American from Mason County. His name eludes me right now, but he'd been around a long time as a member, and he was sergeant-at-arms at the time. He was getting up in years, and he used to doze at his seat. They were discussing this firecracker bill. A fellow by the name of Brig Young—I don't know if you've ever heard the name Brig Young?

I have. Yes.

Well, Brig was a member from Cle Elum. He was the barber who set up Committee Room X. Have you heard of Committee Room X? That's where everyone went for a break at the end of a day. There was a fellow by the name of Max Wedekind who looked like Wallace Beery who played in *Tugboat Annie*. He was a longshoreman from Seattle. I think it was he who had this firecracker and they were passing this firecracker around.

Is this to illustrate the need for the bill?

No. Just some shenanigans. And Brig Young ended up with it. He had a seat, maybe right behind George Adams. Brig put his arm back over his chair with that firecracker in it. Max Wedekind leaned forward with his cigarette lighter and lit that firecracker. Brig heard it fizzling and he gave it a toss. It went right under George Adams' chair and went off. George didn't want to be blamed. Brig was right under the overhang. There were more seats in the chamber then. There are two seats on each side; then there's a third one at the very back. There used to be three along the edge, and they also changed the configuration up front. The press used to sit right in front. They took those seats out and put some of those seats in front. In any case, Brig didn't want to be blamed, so he jumped up out of his seat and looked up …

As though somebody else had done it?

Yes. So Charlie Hodde came down with the speaker's gavel and said, "Any further demonstrations and we'll clear the gallery." That's just a little nonsense that happened.

That's great. The speaker didn't really know what was going on. Had he seen the whole thing?

No. He thought someone from the gallery had thrown it.

Was Hodde as quick with the gavel as others?

I think so.

John O'Brien had that reputation.

O'Brien once slammed it down so hard that the head flew off, almost hitting one of the Republicans in the front row.

What were some other interesting occurrences from the 1949 session?

One thing that passed that session was a big one—I can't remember if it was an initiative on the ballot in '48 or not—but it took two-thirds vote so it must have been. It allowed the City of Tacoma to build the two dams on the Cowlitz River. I remember they had the automatic roll call machine, but they also did an oral vote because they were uncertain about how they were going to come out.

So, 1949 was the Canwell Commission on un-American activities, wasn't it?

That was the session before. That was '47.

What was the perspective or scuttlebutt at that point about Canwell's hunt for alleged communists? He'd probably lost most of his effectiveness, hadn't he?

I think he did. He had his followers but to most people it was kind of a redneck Joe McCarthy type of crusade. I do know they had one of those rooms on the fourth floor with a safe in it and it had a key to a safety deposit box that had all the Canwell hearing papers in it, some of them secret. I don't know why they had that up there, but it was there. Later on when I was assistant chief clerk, I moved it downstairs. I knew about the safe and its controversial contents because in those days they'd have a resolution the first day of the session to buy $75 worth of stamps for each member and I would physically go down and buy those stamps. I'd pick them up and then we would put them in the safe so we'd have someplace other than a cabinet drawer to keep them.

Broad question, but in what ways was the Capitol of that era different from the Capitol of today?

Well, of course the Capitol has come from the horse-and-buggy days to the modern world. Staff for the session used to come out of the Department of Transportation. The committees in the Senate and the House would be staffed from the DOT. The same thing with the budget department, but now we have a good permanent staff.

Why do you say "we"?

I say "we" because I'm still there, in spirit at least. And because I helped develop a lot of it. When I first went there the session was over in 60 days, and it took a little while to get the *Journal* out. Between sessions, the place was locked up; nobody there, no staff.

No tours or anything for the public?

Oh, no. If they did, it wasn't connected with the Legislature. When I first went there the only office the legislators had was their desk on the floor. There were few advantages, but I think one of them was that members were better acquainted with one another. At night you could go in there and oftentimes you could find half of the House reading mail, which they got very little of, or reading bills and so forth. Now the session is over and we have the committee meetings to go to. But they go back to their offices. It used to be they were captive and people came in and talked to them on the floor. That's why the rule in those days was nobody could get on the floor for an hour after adjournment because the members could get something done without lobbyists and people coming in wanting to talk to them.

Do you think camaraderie is lacking now among legislators?

Yeah. Just because of circumstances.

Times sure have changed. What were your duties as assistant chief clerk when you got that job under Si Holcomb in 1957?

They've changed a lot. You've got to realize it was not a modern operation back in those days. You didn't have any permanent staff. You had somebody from the executive office helping pass legislation. You didn't have bill drafting. Both chambers hired bill drafters for the session. Now the Legislature is more on an equal basis than it used to be with the executive and the courts, even though the courts have kind of expanded their authority. People could argue that, I guess.

Decorum has changed, too. Did you dress up for the job everyday, even as an elevator operator?

Oh, yeah.

Shirt and tie?

You bet. Lieutenant Governor John Cherberg was a stickler for the decorum. Sometimes it got pretty warm and some members—like Bob McCaslin from Spokane—would sweat profusely. We would get into a long session and Cherberg would relent, "You can take your jacket off." I remember one time when Booth Gardner was a state senator in the early '70s. It was a Saturday session. Remember when pants were so baggy they looked like they were made from the flour sacks? Gardner came in with a pair of those on. Cherberg almost had a conniption fit. He had Bill Gissberg, another member, talk to him: "Don't come in like that again!" I think decorum is great. It's gotten a bit sloppy, I think, especially in the House.

Society as a whole has gotten sloppy.

Oh, yes. Even at baseball games, everyone had their suits and ties.

Speaking of comparing and contrasting today versus back in the day: The galleries, back in the day, would be a place where people would go to see the action on the floor. I've seen photos and it looks like they're full a lot of the time. And now that isn't the case.

No. They're rarely full.

Why?

I think one reason is that the Senate offices can tune in and hear the action on the Senate floor. I could probably get it piped in to my home if I wanted. So there isn't the demand to be right there when it's happening, you can sit in the comfort of your home or office and listen to what's going on.

Do you think any of the lack of attendance is attributable to apathy as far as the general public is concerned?

Well, I don't know if I'd say it's apathy. How many people can leave their job for a day and go to Olympia? Unless they go to testify. Others realize most of the real work goes on in committees. And usually by the time a bill gets out on the floor, unless it's on the budget or has to do with transportation funding or things like that, they're pretty well settled. I don't know how many votes go through without a dissenting vote. Probably most of them or they have one or two votes against them. The House just goes through them incredibly fast because they have a voting machine. I don't like that because it goes too fast.

There are a few things I wanted to revisit, like your "Tizzy" Tisdale stories. You obviously spent a lot of time with the colorful legislator Clyde V. Tisdale from Pacific County. Same with Bob Bailey, the newspaperman from South Bend who also served in both the House and the Senate. They both left indelible impressions on you. What was your working relationship with those two guys?

I was much closer with Bailey because he ran and beat Ralph Smith two years after Ralph got elected. In fact, the 1951 session is when Bob Bailey

Snyder is sworn into office by Supreme Court Justice Robert Brachtenbach.
Washington State Legislature

Secretary of the Senate Snyder and Reading Clerk Vern Sawyer count roll during
the 1980s. *Washington State Legislature*

went into office. The first day of the session I showed him around. He and his father owned a weekly paper in Raymond. And then he worked as a Linotype operator for *The Aberdeen Daily World*. He was also Congresswoman Julia Butler Hansen's district rep. Bob was highly respected. He was a Senate Democratic caucus chair for years.

Explain to me what the caucus chair does.

He presides over the meeting of caucuses where you discuss bills and any other things that may be pertinent to the Legislature. It's considered the number two leadership position.

Did you hang out with any of the members outside of work?

Oh, yeah. Lots of times I'd be coming from Olympia and stop and visit with Bob Bailey and spend two or three hours there at the Willapa Harbor newspaper.

What about Tizzy?

Not as much. And of course that's when sessions were shorter and there was a longer interim. And that's when I had the store and a young family and all that so there wasn't the opportunity. I can remember Tizzy coming to our house, however, and I can remember him having lunch at our house and visiting. And Bette knew a lot of Tizzy's family and relatives.

They're from Willapa Harbor, too, right?

Yeah. And when little Willapa Valley High School won the state basketball championship in 1936, Bette didn't get to go because she had to stay home with her grandmother. I remember Tizzy saying people in the Valley wouldn't speak to the people in Raymond for several years after that, they were so proud.

You recently honored the surviving members of that team at the Capitol.

We did. What happened was Ken Jacobsen was a state senator for a number of years from Seattle. He was chairman of the Natural Resources committee. Jim Hargrove had Ken come down to Pacific County and hold some meetings and meet with some interest groups from the timber industry and so forth. For some reason we met at Lebam. We told Ken about the 1936 basketball team. So the following Sunday, Ken's neighbor invited him over for a barbecue. Ken explained how he'd come down here and told him about Valley winning the tournament in 1936. The neighbor's dad was there and said, "I was on that team."

There was a Tisdale on that team, too.

Yeah, he was all-state.

Tizzy's brother?

His son. But Ken thought we should do a resolution in the Senate and invited people that were connected with the team. There were only two still living at that time.

One of the most unique aspects of rural areas is that when their sports teams do well they honor it to death. I appreciate that.

I do, too.

Let me ask you about Tizzy and the "tainted money."

That was just a saying. Clyde Tisdale was elected to the House from our district in 1936. He served a couple sessions and then was elected to the Senate. Tizzy called himself a woodsman. He stuttered and he stammered a little bit when he talked. I really think he did it on purpose more than anything else. He ran for Congress and got defeated in the Eisenhower landslide in '52. And then he ran for Congress in '58 and didn't make much of a showing. He was a member of the Communist

Party at one time. He had a lot of sayings and a lot of them were off-color, like a romantic adventure in a hammock. I won't repeat them here. I used to remember a lot of them and I wish I'd have jotted them down. One time something came up and his reply was, "The only trouble with that tainted money is it just t'ain't enough!" Tizzy was always good entertainment, except he repeated himself if he got to drinking a little too much. Somebody said something about getting married again. "W-w-well," he said, "I've been married three times, and I-I think that's enough!" Somebody said, "I should introduce you to my landlady, she's pretty well off." "Well," Tizzy said, "I-I could change my mind. If'n I ever get married again, she's going to have to have a long sock and a bad cough." His adjectives were just out of this world.

That's great!

One morning in 1951, I went over to the Senate with some bills and Lieutenant Governor Vic Meyers was presiding. Meyers said, "For what purpose do you rise, Senator Tisdale? There's nothing before the Senate." Tizzy said, "W-w-well, a point of personal privilege, Mr. President. You know yesterday I was on my feet several times and I-I never did get recognized, and I was beginning to think I was made of celluloid and you were looking right through me. But this morning I'd drunk a couple of cups of black coffee and I see I'm doing better already, thank you." Then one night, the lobbyists were having a few drinks and Tizzy walked in and said to Jack Hurley, a railroad lobbyist, "Mr. Hurley, your railroad engine killed one of my cows one time. I-I never did get compensated for it. Tonight, I'd settle for a couple of drinks of that there Jim Beam." Another time he was kind of holding court, with people standing around listening to him, and he had a drink sitting behind him. He drank straight whiskey, nothing else. No ice, no water, no anything. Tizzy was sipping on this straight whiskey and some young fellow behind him thought Tizzy had had too much to drink. So he took it upon himself to pour a little water in Tizzy's drink. The next sip Tizzy took, he smacked his lips and turned around and said, "Young man, never dilute the spirits with water!"

Any more?

Tizzy was a member in the House of Representatives in 1957, the session where there was a bill to increase legislators' salaries from $10 to $15 a day. He got up and he said, "I-I can remember when they only got $5 a day for the 60 days. We stayed in a room down in the hotel that had a wash basin in it. The toilet and the bath were down the hall. S-s-sometimes the lines were s-s-so long you couldn't wait to get in to take a bath and you had to come up here because there was business going on, and after two or three days you started smelling like a Billy goat. I don't think our constituents want us smelling like Billy goats, so I'm going to vote for this increase to $15 a day, and some of you fellers on the other s-s-side of the aisle who are going to vote no, when the pay whistle blows, you'll trample us to death to get in line to pick up your checks first!" That was Clyde Tisdale. I'll tell one other thing: He was way ahead of his time. You know what he was advocating back in the 1940s and the 1950s? A state lottery. It required a constitutional amendment because the Constitution prohibited games of chance. It takes a two-thirds vote. They were front-page newspaper stories. The galleries were full. The help was all along the edges of the chambers and Tizzy went on for 10, 15, 20 minutes about why the state should have a lottery. Tizzy said, "The Quakers had a lottery to go to war one time, and when you can get the Quakers to go to war you're doing something. People are going to gamble no matter what you think. Whether it's playing Canasta or whatever." And I can remember him saying, "You know sometime somebody's going to stand up on this floor and say 25 other states have a lottery. It's time we have one. Well, it's time we're first. It's time we have one now." A number of years later, the Senate voted on a lottery. But Perry Woodall put an amendment on that said, "This shall be known as the 'Clyde V. Tisdale Lottery.'"

Sounds like a wonderful character.

Like I said, if he'd ever been elected to Congress I think he'd have had an entourage following him around because he was so quotable.

How about August P. "Augie" Mardesich? His "train-leaving-the-platform" story is classic.

I think Augie was as brilliant as Slade Gorton, just a little different. He was a Slav fisherman from Everett who was an attorney. He was around the Legislature a long time—a powerful Democrat. This happened when he was in the House when I was the assistant chief clerk. He had made a speech on a bill. And a fellow by the name of Chuck Moriarity, a Republican from Seattle and another good guy, got up and said, "Do you yield to a question?" Augie said sure. Chuck said, "Representative Mardesich, you've taken the very opposite stance of the Democratic platform. Can you explain your position?" And Augie stood up and said, "As our great Vice President Alben Barkley once said, 'A platform is made to get on the train with. Once you're on the train you don't need the platform anymore.' "

That's deep.

That's Mardesich's mind.

And that was just off the top of his head?

It had to be. He didn't know what question was coming. One morning late in his career while I was still secretary of the Senate, it was getting late in the extra session. It was May. Augie walked in front of the desk. He always had a real brisk walk, almost a half-run. And I'm in my position behind the rostrum. He had a new light-colored suit on. I said, "Good morning, Colonel." He stopped mid stride. He used to lift his glasses up and down. He did that, turned around and said, "There's one big difference: the Colonel deals in chickens, and I deal in pigeons."

That would be Colonel Sanders.

Yep. Augie was accused of kickbacks. He was indicted and went to trial. In fact, I testified at his trial on some technical things. The trial went on for several days. Before the trial, he had to be at the Federal Courthouse in Seattle at 9 a.m. to enter his not-guilty plea. He got back to Olympia at 10:30, and by 11 o'clock—the press, the radio, the TV were all there. In session that day, Augie walked up to the desk. We were on an amendment that was about two-thirds of a page long. Augie said, "Towards the bottom this doesn't read right. There should be a comma between these two words." And I said, "Well, that's part of the code." He said, "I know, but it doesn't read right." So I went back and got the RCW and sure enough whoever had retyped it had left a comma out. Now how, under *any* circumstances, would anybody notice that there was a comma left out between those two words? Especially under those circumstances. I'd have been a blabbering idiot.

The "knives on the table" story is another classic Mardesich tale.

Yes. It must have been 1970. It was a special session and it was getting near the end. They said they were only going to be there 30 days and they stayed 32. R.R. "Bob" Greive, the shrewd Senate majority leader, and Mardesich were sparring. They didn't like each other one bit. We were in the caucus one day, a Saturday. Caucus was about over and Bob was about to drop the gavel to adjourn it and Augie said, "Just a minute. I've got something else I want to talk about. There's a member telling lies about other members of the Senate in my caucus. My father handed down an old Slav custom: 'When you're having trouble with somebody, you walk in and you stick two knives in their desk.'" *Bang! Bang!* There were no knives, but Augie's fists hit the table. About that time there weren't any side conversations going on.

Bet you could have heard a pin drop.

Yeah, you could. And Mardesich said, "When you stick those two knives in the table, you wait for your opponent to grab a knife and you grab yours. You proceed to cut one another up and you start bleeding. Now, you dirty son of a bitch, if I don't get an apology you're going to bleed!"

Then what happened?

Well, Greive jumped up and I think he said some stupid thing. Augie said, "It wasn't that I've supposedly been selling tickets for a fundraiser and skimming some of the money? Or about the franchise bill that went through that I've got payoffs from."

So these were accusations against Mardesich by Greive?

That's right. Greive jumped up and started to say, "Blah, blah, blah, I didn't say anything about you." Or some such thing. And Bob Bailey said, "Caucus adjourned!" He hit the gavel down and everybody filed out. I remember Martin Durkan, another powerful Democrat, was upstairs in his office. I was sitting at my desk when he came out and asked me, "What happened? What happened?" I explained it as much as I could. I was probably shaking. Greive came out of the caucus and walked up to Augie and started talking to him, and I thought they were going to come to fisticuffs. But Senator Don Talley muscled his way between the two of them. I'd never seen Augie that furious before.

Greive had been majority leader for many years, but Mardesich finally dislodged him?

Yeah. He finally got him.

What kept you there all those years, Sid, as both assistant chief clerk with Si Holcomb and then secretary of the Senate?

Intrigue, I guess. The process. For example, the House and the Senate have the right to seat their members. That means somebody may not be seated even if they got elected. I know of two cases. One was in 1933 following the Roosevelt landslide. There were eight Democrats in the 1931 House of Representatives and in 1933 there were 71. And it probably would have been larger except the Democrats didn't have candidates in every race. There was one fellow who was elected as a Democrat. I don't recall his name right now, but he had been convicted of carnal knowledge, I believe it was, between his election and when the Legislature convened. There's very little in the *Journal* about it. I wish there were more, but he was seated and they appointed a special committee to investigate and they reported back that he should be expelled. The members voted to expel him. Then in 1941 there was a gentleman from Snohomish County who did not get sat in the Senate. Lenus Westman was elected to the Senate and was not seated because after the election it came out that he was, or at one time had been, a member of the Communist Party. They had a committee to review the case. One of the members was Al Rosellini. A majority of the committee voted to seat him. Rosellini was one of the minority that voted not to. I was always going to ask him if he can remember why he did that. It was a split vote on the floor, but they voted not to seat him.

So he was not seated?

He was not seated. In later years Westman made a little news once in a while. To my knowledge, those were the only two who weren't seated. And here's a little trivia: one of the members of the House committee in 1933 was Pearl Wanamaker, who was later superintendent of schools.

When somebody like Si Holcomb would, say, teach a class or tell new legislators about the rules, how did he impress on people that this was something important to know?

Si was kind of an icon in my book. When I arrived, it was always "Mr. Holcomb." I never called him Si maybe until much later. And it was "Mr. Hodde" and "Mr. O'Brien." You didn't call people casually by their first names and so forth. When Si conducted these classes he—I don't want to say exemplified—but he had a position of authority and he was a person who reflected that authority. I think people listened and took an interest. When I first came there the place was a lot quieter because the only two people who had a microphone were the reading clerk and the speaker. So when people got up to speak you had to be quiet to listen to them.

Would they go take the microphone?

No, they spoke from their seats without a microphone.

So there was a sense of decorum. It that lost today?

Yes. Decorum and dignity and respect. The respect for one another, even though these were cantankerous times.

Some people are good parliamentarians and others are not. Is that a natural skill or is it something you have to really work at?

I think it's a little bit of both. It was stressed. You should know the rules and you should know how they work. Working as assistant chief clerk and secretary of the Senate for 31 years, you naturally are going to know the rules.

Bob Greive once said he had flash cards that had all the parliamentary rules on them. I wondered about other people, though. For example, when you learned parliamentary procedure was it just repetitiveness or is it something you really had to study and understand the underlying structure?

I think it was study. And also the biggest thing was the experience you earned as you went along. I remember Bob Greive's flash cards, certainly. He had those and he used them greatly to his advantage. But there were other people around in those years who were, I think, great parliamentarians, too. And then there are people who really don't care much about the rules. You had Mardesich and Gissberg, and you had Marshall Neill, who was a Republican. You had Frank Atwood and John Ryder, who were both Republicans. They knew the rules pretty well. They differed sometimes on interpretation and that's where you got long delays. John Cherberg would put the Senate at ease and go back in his office. It would usually be John Cherberg, myself and his attorney. One of the most common rulings was made on the scope and object. You offer an amendment to a bill and one of the ploys would be that a member would get up and say the amendment expands the scope and object of the bill, which it can't do. So the person who made the motion on scope and object would explain why they thought it expanded the scope and object. Then the person who submitted the amendment would usually get up and give his reasons. Oftentimes, we'd go back and discuss it. John Crowley from Spokane was Cherberg's attorney for several years. We'd all put in our thoughts and then Crowley would write the ruling. Crowley did most of the advising. Sometimes when you'd say "It can go either way," John Cherberg would say, "I'm going to rule for my friends." He made people mad. I can remember Senator Bud Shinpoch, a hardnosed Democrat, being really upset at him because he ruled against him one time.

Was there always an attorney with the speaker and the chief clerk in the House?

Yes. In the later years, Marty Brown was the lieutenant governor's attorney. Now there are two attorneys on the rostrum. One from each caucus. I'm not particularly fond of that idea because I think they can get a little too political in their advice to the lieutenant governor. I think the lieutenant governor should have his own attorney.

Take somebody like Si Holcomb. Would he be more familiar with parliamentary procedure than say, whoever was the speaker at that time, Charlie Hodde or John O'Brien?

Probably, even though Hodde was speaker twice. John was there four sessions. I think John studied the rules a lot more than the others did.

Did your relationship with Holcomb change over time? I wonder how your relationship evolved.

I think it continued to be very good. I can't remember any disagreements with Si, and if there were, they were very minor. I know sometimes he wouldn't be there. I'd have to go down to the hotel room and get him to sign some documents that he needed to sign.

But generally speaking he had become, even if he didn't get along with John O'Brien, such an institution the speaker wouldn't have considered removing him?

Si had a lot of good friends, yes. He had a lot of great friends. And you do, you establish friends as you go along there. One thing, especially in the earlier years, I was so involved in my work that I never really got into the politics of things as much as I would have liked to now—if I could go back and look at those things.

So your focus had to be so much on how things were running?

Yes. And I never went to committee meetings to listen. Maybe on the floor you listened sometimes, but you're always doing things. Maybe somebody was talking to you about helping them with an amendment or something else or back into the workroom, back and forth, so you never really did get to sit and enjoy the debate that was going on. And I was probably a little naïve, too.

Tell me a little bit about how your relationship with individual legislators worked.

We were there to serve the members and we served them any way we could. If they'd want help that we could provide, we did. It was just that simple. I don't think there were any real brainy things that went into it. Sometimes they'd ask about procedures. A lot of them weren't interested in procedures. They were interested in getting things done. But they would get to a point and say, "Hey, maybe I need some help. What's going to happen here?"

Generally, would that be younger members?

Probably to some extent. Every year that probably diminished a little bit. I can remember one night being invited by a group of senators to Johnny's Dock Restaurant in Tacoma when they used to serve white-gloved dinners in their basement. And I wasn't even a House member. I was the only House associate there. I seemed to get along well with people and I think that helped a lot.

John O'Brien was a powerful and controversial speaker. Did he have any kind of working relationship with you as assistant chief clerk?

Yes. We had a working relationship. I don't think it was anything overwhelming. I got along with him well, I thought. But you've got to remember most of the time we saw him he was on the rostrum or when we took the bills in for final assignment. He's got 98 members who are after him for his time and he's meeting with members to plan how in the hell they are going to get this session over with. John was a loner. Instead of going down in the lunchroom and having lunch, he'd have his lunch brought up and sit and eat in the office by himself. I think he would have done himself a lot more good if he'd have mingled a little more. But that was just my opinion. I never gave it to him, and he never asked me for it.

I know there were plans to expand the Capitol Campus during the 1950s.

There was a plan at one time to tear down the Institutions Building [now the Irv Newhouse Building]. I think they wanted to put up a 25-story building there. I'm sure it was over 20. John Cherberg is the one who defeated that idea. They were going to move the governor's office over there and keep a ceremonial office in the Capitol building. When Pete von Reichbauer switched parties in 1981, there were, I think, about two or three Democrats in the Institutions Building and the rest of them were Republicans. John Jones, who was the minority caucus chairman, became the majority caucus chairman. He asked me to move the Democrats out of there. So they had all the Democrats in one building and the Republicans in the other. I've always regretted that because I think it helps if you have a mixture and have people next door to one another. I know it was cumbersome and it would never work today, but when the only office the members had were their desks on the floor, I think they got better acquainted with one another because oftentimes up to half the members would come back in the evening to work at their desks and there would be little rump caucuses going on with a half-dozen members in one place and maybe some down in the cafeteria. They'd be down there having coffee or ice cream or a snack and sitting around visiting. Now, once the session's over, everybody rushes away from the floor and back to their offices or to a committee meeting.

Just another place to interact.

Yes. When Ted Bottiger, a Democrat from Tacoma, was the majority leader, on a certain night of the week, he would have the press in for a cocktail and he'd sit around and visit with them and they'd ask him questions. Oftentimes, there were other members there. Here again, I think that was a plus. When he quit serving drinks nobody showed up.

How much input might you have as assistant chief clerk into the development of the campus and the offices and how they were used and those types of things?

We really had quite a bit. In '65 when Bob Schaefer was speaker, we had this committee that went around the United States and looked at what they'd done in different states. We put offices in the fourth floor of what is now the O'Brien Building and the Cherberg Building. Most of the Senate members had private offices. Most of the House offices were shared by two members. A few members shared in the Senate, too, and there were some House members on the top floor of the Cherberg Building. I was in on the planning of those, even down to assigning who got different offices. But always with the approval of somebody else. I've always been involved in planning projects. There were several before that and several since then. As a member, I didn't get as deeply involved in that as I'd like to, because I just had too many other things to do.

Because there wasn't permanent staff did you end up filling a lot of duties that ultimately were parceled out amongst permanent staff when they arrived?

Oh, I think so. Yes. We delivered the bills to the governor's office and got receipts for them. That duty has passed on to somebody else now.

So you were the jack-of-all-trades of the House?

Yes.

How did the Joint Interim Committee on Facilities and Operations get started? Did it start with the fact that everybody was on the floor, or was it just later?

I just think they found out the way they were doing things was cumbersome. I think it was only natural to think, "Hey, we're coming of age here." It was kind of a horse-and-buggy Legislature that had become a weak third branch of the government. So they needed to update their facilities and their equipment and so on.

When you were on this interim committee, or served with it, you actually went and visited other states?

Yes. It was one trip and it included several states. It was New Mexico which had recently come up with offices, and two or three other states. Maybe it was North Carolina and South Carolina. I know we went to Texas. In Texas, the lieutenant governor and the speaker had apartments in the Legislative Building.

Were there any states in particular that ultimately Washington modeled itself after?

There were other states that came out to see what had happened in Washington.

I meant when the Legislature went on to make some changes and decisions about buildings and office spaces. Was what was done in Washington modeled after something you saw on that trip?

I think they just picked out things from things around. And then of course there have been several remodels and they're still going on today in the Cherberg Building. They finally took over the whole building. That's when they built the Natural Resources Building and moved that office down there. Members were always reluctant to do anything for themselves because they got criticized every time they spent money on such things.

I read something that suggested at one time they actually thought about tearing down the Governor's Mansion and putting an apartment complex in where there would be apartments for legislators and a penthouse for the governor.

I remember when they talked about tearing the mansion down. I don't remember talk of putting any apartments there for the members. I think the big change was 1973 when Len Sawyer was speaker of the House, and Augie Mardesich was majority leader. That's when they eliminated most of the interim committees. They had one on fisheries, one on game, or maybe that was a combination. There was one on higher education, one on education, one on regulatory reform. The big one was the Legislative Council. Then they staffed the standing committees in the interim. I may have mentioned before that Jim Bricker was the chief staff person on the Higher Education Interim Committee prior to 1973. And Cathy Wolfe worked on the committee and there was one other lady who worked on the committee. I can't remember her name. But that was what most of them had, two or three staff people.

This was the same time a year-round Legislature was being proposed, too, right?

Yes. I know in my situation, when I was a member, I always thought it was healthy for me to get back and visit with the local service clubs and chambers and schools and just the people in the store. Sometimes you were surprised when some people that you think wouldn't even know the Legislature was going on would stop and have a conversation with you. On the other hand, there were people you think would be knowledgeable who weren't. But one of these days it will probably change, and it probably has to a great extent because there are very few legislators anymore who have a fulltime additional career when they're not in session. I think at one time the Senate was about half attorneys. And the House was probably 25 percent or more attorneys. So that meant there were 50 attorneys in the Legislature. I know it's down to less than 10 now, maybe less than five, and probably very few are practicing.

I would think many of them are retired.

Yes. And that's the way with a lot of the members of the Legislature. They're retired teachers or maybe they're young and just getting started. Their wife has an income, and with the legislative salary they can get by for a while, but then they drop out. I've had some younger members in the Legislature come and talk to me and say, "Why should I stay? I'm gone all the time, or most of the time. I have children and I miss their piano recitals and their concerts and their sporting events and their spelling bees and things like that, and I don't know if it's worth it or not." Plus the beating you take from the public in general and from the press and special interest groups. It's hard to find members to run for the Legislature.

As a staff member who was there longer than most of the legislators, you were in the same position of being away for a good amount of time. Didn't that also apply to some of the long-term staff?

Yes. But in those early years when I was secretary of the Senate it was just session time and then nothing until the next session came around. In between, there were a few functions. Really, until 1973, it didn't get to be a year-round job, and even then I was a part-time employee for those early years. Can I interject here with a story I'm thinking of?

Of course.

Jack Williams was one of the gentlemen who came from a family that founded Ilwaco. Jack had a great, dry sense of humor. When I first started in business the only bank in town was in Ilwaco, just a couple miles from Seaview. I'd go down to the bank and Jack was oftentimes across the street from the bank and holding court with four or five, six, eight, ten people. Invariably, Jack would motion me across the street, and I was dressed like I am today, shirt sleeves and no jacket. He'd say, "You know, my brother Reese and I are very influential in the Republican Party, and if you can get yourself a jacket, we just might be able to get you elected governor. And if he said that once he said it 150 times. One day he walked by me in the store said, "Sid, you know that Dixy Lee Ray? I think you can beat her without a jacket!"

Tell me about the budget and accounting act.

My first session as assistant chief clerk was 1957 and they had been accustomed to stopping the clock. That session was Al Rosellini's first as governor and he decided to get it over in 60 days. We worked practically all night every night to get out of there. Then the next session the act was passed. And I think the biggest part of that was that you have to have a balanced budget. Now in those days you didn't have such a good forecast. You didn't have experts like Dr. Chang Mook Sohn and others I served with on the Revenue Forecast Council when I was a senator. I think there was a little adjusting of the revenue outlook to fit the budget. But that was the start of it. That was the year they passed the administrative procedures act.

Why was Governor Rosellini so insistent on ending in 60 days, whether the budget was determined or not?

You realize he'd only been in office 58 days when the 60th day came. Getting your feet on the ground, making cabinet appointments. He had all that hanging over his head. All the bills that the Legislature had passed that he had to look forward to signing or vetoing or partially vetoing. He thought, or his handlers thought, or members of the leadership thought, "Let's get out of here. The best thing we can do is to go home and work on it next time." Now that's me talking, that's not Al Rosellini or any of his people.

But from your perspective, what did you think about the fact that the budget was sort of left up in the air. I mean the fact that it wasn't balanced.

It wasn't balanced, but I don't think it was out of balance much. Of course what would the balanced budget have been in 1957?

Compared to modern days.

Was it a billion or two then? I don't really recall right now.

Did the provisions of the budget and accounting act come from the governor's office primarily?

I think he had a governor's request bill.

The whole notion of a balanced budget, how would that affect your job in terms of the chief clerk's office and the Senate secretary's office?

It didn't. The Legislature in those years used to pass its own budget at the beginning of the session. That changed over the years. As secretary of the Senate, I'd sit down with the ladies in our accounting office and determine how much money we'd spent the previous biennium or the current biennium and determine how much we were going to spend. We would try to guess the likelihood of having a special session, and then come up with a figure. Of course, the Legislature could always add more if it needed to, which we didn't like to do. It seemed like the House—of course they had more members to deal with—had to come in with supplemental appropriations a few times. But we just passed a bill at the end of the session. Si always used to try to pick a day when something else was going on. Maybe as early as the third day if it was an inauguration day. So it wouldn't be front-page news, it would be on one of the inside sections—because when they don't have anything to write about they are writing about how much money it's going to cost to operate the Legislature. We even had a bill for how much money each member was going to get for stamps.

The stamps story is a good one. Tell me that one again.

It was customary to pass certain bills the first few days of the session. One of them was to authorize the Association of Washington Business to do the digest for us. A separate bill was to allow each member so much for stamps. You've got to remember we were pretty antiquated. You didn't have phones at your desks or anything like that. I think the House had two WATS lines for long-distance calls. I went down to the post office and bought rolls of stamps, whatever denominations they were, and we passed them out to all the members and had the members sign for them. That was a big deal.

And later there was what you call the "stamp act."

Yes. Somebody like Bob Bailey, who didn't do a lot of mass mailings, we just kept adding to his account. If he got $5,000 and used $1,000, then he had a $4,000 balance. The next year, he got $5,000 and used $1,000 and he had an $8,000 balance. Someone wrote an article on it and there was a big to-do over it. I didn't go on a Cherberg trade mission because of the stamp act and the big investigation going on. Bob got appointed to the Utilities and Transportation Commission and he drew out his stamp allowance, which was $12,000 or something. A lot of senators, like Reuben Knoblauch, had huge amounts. They interviewed a lot of members and employees and I think Senator Gordon Herr was fined a small amount and that was the only thing that came out of it. But it was big news.

So Bob Bailey's $12,000, for example, was that just his pocket money if he didn't use it for postage?

He could use it any way he wanted to. But there was never anybody more honest than Bob Bailey. Everyone had their stamp money. It was Democrats, Republicans, House members, Senate members.

The 1951 special session certainly was interesting.

That year, the Legislature passed the budget and they put a tax in the budget. The Constitution says that you can only have one subject matter in a bill. Vic Meyers was lieutenant governor and the presiding officer at the time and somebody put this tax measure up. Somebody raised the point of order that it was beyond the scope and object of the bill. And Vic Meyers ruled that it was. Somebody made a motion to overrule the chair. This is virtually unheard of. And they voted to overrule and the amendment stayed in the bill. I believe it increased the liquor taxes, which it usually did. Anytime there was a tax measure on tobacco and liquor, the distilleries would file a suit that it was unconstitutional. This time, there were two subjects in one bill. In August, the Supreme Court ruled in favor of Meyers. Vic used to say he was the only presiding officer who had ever had his ruling upheld by the Supreme Court. So the state was broke. It didn't have any money. The bill was thrown out, so they had a special session to correct that in September of '51. That was one that lasted two or three days. I came for that little bit of that session. And I'll tell another story to follow up on that: The Republicans had control in 1997 and passed a transportation bill, put a referendum on it, and it had bonds—a lot of things in it. So I raised a point of order that it had more than one subject in it. It was getting close to the end of the session. Brad Owen was lieutenant governor. I remember going out in the rotunda into the state reception room and a lobbyist said, "What's holding up the Senate?" And I explained that I had raised a point of order because there was more than one subject, and she said, "There's more than one subject in that all right." Well, Brad and his attorneys ruled against me.

So it went to the ballot. I forget all the details, but if that hadn't gone to the ballot it would have changed the whole way the transportation thing ended up going. You can disagree, but you don't argue with the presiding officer. And we were in the minority. Overruling him would have triggered another hassle. I thought I had a lead-pipe cinch on my ruling that day.

Increasing liquor taxes seemed to be a common move. Wasn't there once a tax on pop bottles that upset many?

In 1957, they decided they'd go home and pass a tax bill in '59 or maybe it ended up being in '61. Maybe they raised the sales tax one-third of a cent or increased the tax on tobacco and liquor. Also they had a one-cent bottle tax on soda pop. That's before there were cans. The bill got over to the House and the bottlers all became upset. That's when every small community had its own bottler. Raymond had an outfit called the Dennis Company that bottled root beer and orange and cream under a Dennis Company label. Cammarano Brothers, I think, in Olympia had one. Anyhow, these people all showed up to lobby the House against the pop tax. If I recall, most of them were driving white Cadillacs. But the strange thing was that O'Brien had a lot of these people as clients of his accounting firm. Anyhow, the governor, Al Rosellini, had to have the bill as is, no changes. Well, we got out on the floor and somebody put up an amendment to strike the section that established the pop tax. As was customary in those days, they asked for a division of the house—a standing vote. Now if they ask for a division in the House they automatically get a roll call vote. In the Senate it's still a count. And as was customary in those days, I counted the left-hand side. Si counted the right-hand side. I'd give him my vote. He'd total them. Then the nays would stand. We followed that procedure and it kind of looked like the nays had it, but Si juggled the totals and turned around and handed it to O'Brien. It was a tie vote. The pop bottlers are in the first row of the gallery waiting for the decision. O'Brien looked at the vote count, and glanced up in the gallery. He used to get a pained look just like he'd had a gas attack. And of course Rosellini was from his legislative district. He took a deep breath and voted no and the pop tax stayed in the bill. It got down to the governor's office and Rosellini vetoed it. It was a crime to put a tax on those poor kids. So Si put O'Brien right through the wringer on that tax.

What was Holcomb's motivation?

I don't know what it was.

I wanted to talk a little about the '61 session. That was the year O'Brien had the first real strong challenge to his speakership. It was his fourth term and all of a sudden he had some fairly strong opposition. Leonard Sawyer was, I think, the primary person to challenge him from within his own party. Can you tell me a little bit about the process to select the speaker as session nears?

Sometime between the general election in November and the start of the session, each of the four caucuses has an organizational caucus. The majority party in the House elects the speaker. The minority elects their minority leader and the other positions. Then there's a speaker pro-tem. The majority party elects the secretary of the Senate and the sergeant-at-arms. I don't know if the House elects the sergeant-at-arms anymore. The Senate majority's caucus elects a majority leader, which is almost equivalent to what the speaker is, except the Constitution provides that the lieutenant governor is the presiding officer in the Senate. Then the minority party also elects its officers.

Now, the organizational caucuses usually come as close to the general election as possible. Sometimes they have to postpone them because they don't know who's going to be in control. The Senate has had several 25-24 majorities the last few years. In 1961, there were 59 Democrats elected and their organizational caucus was held in one of the House committee rooms right off of the floor. At that time all the House and the Senate members were primarily lodged on the third and fourth floors. I wasn't inside the caucus room. There was one member absent. I can't remember his name. He was a schoolteacher from Olympia. By that time he may have been a retired school teacher, but he was on vacation, so it left 58 members. I think all four caucuses have rules that determine how many votes it takes to get elected. For the Senate Democrats, I know, for the last number of years, it takes a majority of those elected to the Senate to be elected to any of the caucus positions. In those days it was just a majority of those who were present at the meeting. So with 58 members there it took 30.

When they took a vote it was 29-29. I don't know how many votes they took, but it was 29-29 every time. They would break and have little rump caucuses between each vote. Finally, Sawyer withdrew and Augie Mardesich's name was placed in nomination. Also as a test vote they had me running against Si Holcomb, and it still ended up 29-29. I didn't know that until later. But that was just a test vote to see how things would come out.

Mardesich had been the floor leader of the Democrats the session before.

Under O'Brien, yes. I'll go back and if I tell a little story here I hope you don't mind.

Not at all.

In 1955, it was 50 Democrats, 49 Republicans. Julia Butler Hansen, a Democrat from Cathlamet, ran for speaker. At that time, Gordon Sandison of Port Angeles and Augie Mardesich were kind of O'Brien lieutenants. I wasn't there at that time, but they were going around getting votes for O'Brien. O'Brien won 27-23 in the caucus. After the vote, Julia Butler Hansen walked up to Sandison and said, "No hard feelings, but I'll get even, you son of a bitch!" That's the way Julia talked. A very tough lady. She would have been the first woman speaker of the House.

Now to fast forward to '61: I don't know why Mardesich was supporting Sawyer at that time, but Mardesich put his name up instead of Sawyer's, and the vote was 31-27 in favor of O'Brien. Customarily, everybody votes to support the person that won. A lot of the Sawyer people were very upset with Clayton Farrington—*that was the teacher's name*—because he wasn't at the caucus. I don't know if he was gone on purpose or if he was committed to both people and didn't want to be there or what it was. But anyhow, that's how close it was to unseating O'Brien in 1961.

Can you tell me a little bit about Sawyer's position? Why did he want to unseat O'Brien?

I don't know. Of course the speaker position carries a lot of authority and a lot of power. I think a lot of people dream about being speaker. I don't know what his motive or his plan was. To my knowledge, prior to that, speakers usually only served one term. There was an exception. There was a gentleman by the name of Ed Riley from Spokane. I believe he served two sessions as speaker but not consecutively. There were two Ed Rileys in the Legislature, by the way. The other was from Seattle, and somebody came up with monikers. They called Ed Riley from Seattle "Saltwater Ed" and Ed Riley from Spokane "Freshwater Ed."

"Freshwater Ed" had been the speaker, then?

Yes.

Did you have a sense within the caucus or within the House as a whole that there was the desire to have some kind of turnover and new leadership?

Oh, I think maybe it was just kind of like with George Washington only serving two terms, and nobody ever served more than two until Roosevelt. I think it was more of a precedent than anything.

I am curious about your take on another reason some people give for O'Brien's decline in power. That it in part was because Julia Butler Hansen was gone. Does that seem possible to you that the fact that she had gone to Congress and wasn't there to help solidify his supporters?

Yes. She left in '60 for Congress so she wasn't there in that '61 session. I couldn't say that for sure, but I think that's a pretty good theory. Yes, I think she and O'Brien were pretty good friends, really.

There was one story from this period about Wes Uhlman going up to the dome of the Capitol and hiding from a vote or something until the sergeant-at-arms found him.

That could have been. But any member can get up and say, "I demand a call of the House." So the presiding officer says—maybe they take a vote first—"Lock the doors!" So they lock everybody in. I've known people to sneak out some way or go and hide. P.J. Gallagher from Tacoma used to do that. It's usually pretty hard for somebody to get out. But the difference is when you don't have a "call," which they seldom do anymore, when you call roll if you come to Jones and Jones isn't in his seat, you go to the end of the roll and come back. Members come in and vote from the edge of the chambers. You'll see them do that.

When you're under the call of the House or the Senate, when you come to Jones and if he hasn't been excused from the call, you wait until he is found, until he comes in and votes. He or she. Now there are times when you wait a moment or two, somebody might be in the bathroom or something like that. I know P.J. Gallagher used to go back and hide maybe in the assistant chief clerk's office or the chief clerk's office. That was in later years when we had offices. And maybe Wes did get out and get up in the dome.

Another incident I remember was when the Senate thought the session was over and, here again is another little trivia story from when Rosellini was governor. It used to be customary they had resolutions up at the top of the order of business. The minority party would put a resolution in to kind of criticize something, and the Republicans would put a resolution in to criticize. One time, they put one in to criticize Rosellini. The customary thing was that the majority party just makes a motion to lay it on the table. That cuts off all debate and they can't have a vote and that's the end of it.

Bob Bailey was the caucus chair, and as he told the story, they put this resolution up and Bob Greive looked over at him and wanted to know, "What the hell?" you know. So they went ahead and adopted it on a voice vote. And Rosellini was quite upset. On the last day of the session when everything was pretty well over, the governor insisted that they put a resolution in to expunge that from the record.

I remember Perry Woodall was having a heyday, saying, "How do you erase something that's actually happened?" If I remember right, Davy Cowen and Jim Keefe had headed for the airport to fly back to Spokane and they had a call of the Senate. So they had to send the sergeant-at-arms out to bring them back to vote on expunging the record. I don't think they actually expunged the record. I think they came to some other solution. But they were pretty irate because they had to come back for that.

In the '61 session, Governor Rosellini introduced a proposal whereby he would essentially appoint a whole new liquor control board?

I don't remember any details. I remember that happening and that's about all.

You had mentioned earlier about the tax on the soft drinks, and my sense is that something similar happened with this liquor control board issue, and that the liquor people were in there. I've heard that they sometimes spread the liquor around pretty liberally to members.

Yes. And I think a lot of that went on even earlier than what we're talking about. They used to say, "That's a two-case bill" or "That's a one-case bill" or something like that. Another trivia story here: At the end of one of the sessions the lobbyists had promised Vic Meyers a case of Scotch or whiskey or whatever it was, and they pulled in the garage to put it in the trunk of his Cadillac. But they actually put in into the trunk of a fellow from Whatcom County by the name of Ernie Leonard. I think he was a Swedish immigrant because he talked quite broken. Ernie was a teetotaler, even though I think his family had breweries in Sweden. It was the day after the session and he was heading home. When he got north of

Olympia near Fort Lewis he got a flat tire. Ernie was an older gentleman and he had quite a bad limp. He got out to fix the tire and some soldier from Fort Lewis stopped to help him. And so here's this case of Scotch in the trunk. Ernie didn't know how it got there, so he gave it to the soldier for helping him fix the tire.

During the famous coalition-related speaker coup in 1963, it sounds like you had a pretty good relationship with Republican leadership. Obviously they had the backing of their caucus to hatch this plot to topple O'Brien, didn't they?

Oh, yes. After William "Big Daddy" Day, a Democrat from Spokane, was elected speaker by the Dan Evans coalition, O'Brien got up and made some angry speeches. Day was on the rostrum and he came close to gaveling O'Brien down a couple of times. And I worked with the coalition quite a bit that first week. In fact, when the session was finally over they came in. Si and I both worked with them. And I worked with Slade Gorton, a key member of the Evans group, during that week. He wanted to change the rules. He had gone over them thoroughly and made a lot of changes. If you look at the red manual on legislative procedures, some of them were quite obvious. Of course we did session hiring, and that's all there was in those days.

Bob Perry, one of the Democrats who conspired with the Republicans, took exception to some of the people who were even coming in as pages for the first two or three weeks. Bob was a very intelligent guy. I think he's the one who really engineered the coalition by making an overture to Gorton. But he even wanted to not bring in some of the pages who had been scheduled because of who their sponsors were.

Tell me a little bit more about him, because Bob Perry seems to be, at least to some people, a mystery figure.

He is kind of a mystery figure. He was accused of kick-back schemes. He certainly knew how to run elections and campaign. I know one thing he always did: He clipped the obituaries out of the paper, anybody in his district and he'd take them off his mailing list. That was before they could buy all of the lists and so forth. Bob was a very bright guy.

And his strong feelings in terms of the coalition, where did they come from?

I'm quite sure it was the public-private power fight. He was from West Seattle.

But he seemed to be, from your perspective, one of the leading coalitionists?

He's the one who had the brights, and I don't mean to say cunning, but you know he could figure things out, how to get them done. He had forged a curious friendship with Gorton.

Did it put you in a difficult position having to balance everything?

I just went on doing my job like I thought I should be doing, and if people asked me for advice I would give it to them. If they asked me questions, I'd try to answer them and be as fair as I could. It's kind of like bill drafting. You go down and ask for a bill to be drafted, the bill drafter can't say, "Well, so-and-so is drafting the same bill, I thought you'd like to know that." Or that somebody's drafting one just the opposite.

I think that issue of integrity is what obviously distinguished you.

I don't know about that, but…

Another thing I have read, and again I wanted to just throw this out and see what your reaction was, is that there were some Democrats who made accusations that possibly private power was influencing the vote perhaps by making some significant donations to campaigns and things like that. Did you have any sense of that?

I wasn't that involved in campaigns and campaigns weren't that involved with money. I can remember when a fellow by the name of Ray Olsen, who was later sergeant-at-arms, was a member from Seattle. I think he spent $5,000 on a campaign and that was just mind-boggling. Maybe $100 or $500 would have been a large amount, but there was no public disclosure at that time to really find out how much money did go into those campaigns.

During that 1963 session, how did Speaker Day deal with the Republican interests and the rest of the Democratic interests? Was it pretty much down the line every issue?

I don't think so. I thing there were undoubtedly times when he ruled with the coalitionists, but, no, I don't think it was down the line. There may have been bills, and I'm sure there were, that had Democratic sponsors that didn't pass just because their name was on it. But why make somebody upset by not letting their bill out and get over to the Senate and pass? They were probably saying, "Well here's member X from a certain district. A Republican isn't going to beat him or we're not going to beat him with another Democrat, so why not try to make a friend out of him instead of irritating him because sometime we may need his vote?" I don't know what they were looking at in the '65 session, but Day didn't run for speaker, Bob Schaefer did and won. But, sure, there were a lot of hard feelings and a lot of bills didn't get passed because of who sponsored them. But a lot of them did pass. I remember Day saying, "We're not going to have a committee on revenue and taxation because we're not going to have any tax increases."

Was there a problem with decorum? Did Day find that it was hard sometimes to keep members in line?

I don't think anything out of the ordinary. I don't recall any spats just because it was a coalition. That's not saying there wasn't.

They did reduce the number of House committees, right? You mentioned the revenue and taxation, but wasn't there an overall plan to reduce them some?

They did reduce the committees. Of course, O'Brien's plan was that every Democrat, except freshman members, either were on Rules Committee or had a chairmanship. So he had to expand and reduce the amount of committees according to how many fell in that category. I think we had 25 or 30 committees. If you look now there are about a dozen. It used to be you never had times set for committee meetings. The committee chairman would get up and announce the meetings. Members were on a lot more committees. Sometimes a member would be on two or three committees meeting at the same time. But now it's much better organized and the time slots are set.

So really committee creation to a degree was a reward for the majority to...

To accommodate, yes. And some of them maybe only had three or four bills a session.

Did the Democratic coalitionists continue to stick together? They were the outcasts from their regular caucus.

In terms of work, I don't think there was too much intermingling between the coalitionists and the regular Democrats. Not that there wasn't some. There may have been a few of the regular Democrats who would have liked to have voted for Day but didn't. I can't prove that point, but I'm sure there would have been some.

Was it more contentious after the coalition?

I think it was. They were trying to make a record for themselves or get somebody on the record so they might be able to use it in a campaign against them. I think most of the time most of those things are very ineffective. It goes on today. It will probably go on forever.

Here's a hypothetical situation: There's a bill out, maybe on heavier sentences for sex offenders. Maybe the Republicans would put up an amendment to increase the sentences. I'm opposed to the amendment not just because of the cost of incarceration, but because I'd rather try treatment. So I vote against the amendment and in the next election they say, "Sid Snyder is soft on sex offenders." Both parties do things like that. Sid Snyder wasn't soft on sex offenders. He voted for the final bill.

Maybe a better example would be drug addicts. If they're going to put somebody in jail for two or three years and not give them any treatment, I'd rather reduce their sentence and put them in a rehab program to try to get them straightened out so they're not back in prison six months or a year or six weeks after they're let out.

Tell me more about the public versus private power debate.

Legislation was passed in the mid- to late-1930s to establish the PUDs— Public Utility Districts. A fellow by the name of Guy C. Meyers was behind it. He was from back east someplace and ended up arranging for the financing on Wall Street with projects, such as the Rocky Reach Dam. I think that was one of the last ones he financed. At that time it was about $225 million, and he got one-quarter of 1 percent or one-eighth of 1 percent. His daughter lived in Long Beach. Guy Meyers put in a huge cranberry bog down there before and after World War II.

Did he have ties to the Grange?

I don't know if he did.

I know the Grange also was really instrumental in getting the PUDs started.

Oh, yes. Absolutely.

How do you assess the importance of this sort of the whole public versus private power debate in terms of Washington history?

I think it's a whopping issue and I don't know if it's going to be an issue in the future or not. I don't think to the same extent. I think if you tried to form a PUD to take over a private power company you'd have an awfully tough time doing that today.

Because of the size and the cost of doing it?

Yes. The money that would be spent. But that was before a lot of people had electricity and it was expensive. Rural electrification, I think, was the reason the Grange was in it.

There are those who suggest that was the most important issue in Washington history.

I wouldn't disagree with that.

I don't think people today realize the extent of the political divisions that it caused over time. Maybe people in rural areas do, but certainly I don't get a sense that it's a burning issue for anybody.

People forget so fast, I know. People say, "John Cherberg? Who's John Cherberg?" How many people have never heard of him? He was a household name for decades.

I'd like to talk more about the progressive Republicans who came to power during the 1960s. Bob Greive used to call them the "tennis court" Republicans. Did people early on begin to see these new Republicans as a force to be reckoned with?

I think people saw them. There were a lot of people who came into the Legislature in '57 and '59, both Democrats and Republicans. But more of the Republicans ended up later being statewide officers or other officers. Dan Evans came to the House in '57. Slade Gorton came in '59. Joel Pritchard came in '59. Of course Evans we know was governor and a U.S. senator and Slade was attorney general and a U.S. senator and got beaten then got re-elected. And Joel was a state senator and in Congress for several years and then he was a representative to the U.N. Then he came back as lieutenant governor. So he had quite a career.

Those people and a lot of others were referred to as "Dan Evans Republicans." There were quite a few of them. And there were others who came along about that same time. Wes Uhlman was a freshman in '59, I think he was 23-years-old. And of course he ended up as mayor of Seattle, and he almost ended up as governor. Dixy Lee Ray beat him by a few votes.

Committee Room X, the controversial storage closet turned social hangout also had a barbershop element.

It was a service for the members. Especially when it first started. They didn't have 50 cents for a haircut or six bits for a shave and a haircut. Was that the old saying? It was convenient because members' time was at a premium and to get out and get your hair cut took a lot of time. For several years, they did have a place in the House to fix the ladies' hair, too.

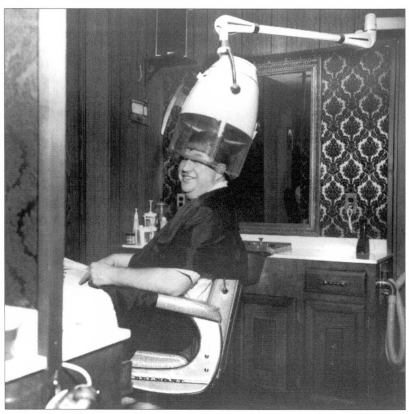

Snyder sits under the hairdryer in Rags Thornton's salon at the Capitol.

Where was that?

Right off the House floor on the south side. It was originally the ladies' lounge. They could go in and get the whole works done.

But Committee Room X had that social element until Don Miles came along and pushed for its closure as part of his campaign in 1962. Why did he do that?

You'd have to ask Don Miles that question. But if I remember right, Don was a teetotaler and of course if the general public thinks half-drunks are passing their laws … But do we get any better legislation today than we did in those years? I don't think so. In fact, when everything is right out in the open and so forth, it's pretty hard to vote against interest groups sometimes. So I just think it was an issue that didn't sit well with the public. People don't want drunk drivers. They don't want drunken legislators. There may have been excessive drinking in the Legislature back 50 years ago. I certainly don't think there is now.

It wasn't uncommon at all that when five o'clock came a lot of members would have happy hour in their offices. To most people that sounds like a way to not pass legislation. But it was another way people got acquainted with one another and then found out that maybe someone is a pretty good guy, you know. He's on the level. I think in the old days, too, if a fellow was from a certain industry or a certain type of business, and if he got up and said something, you believed him. You just relied on somebody who was a commercial fisherman. They become the expert. Dick Kink was a commercial fisherman and if he got up and people had confidence in him, confidence in what he said, that was it.

Did members ever vote drunk?

I think it was a rarity. One thing was members used to break for dinner and then come back in the evening. Members would go out and have dinner and have a few drinks and come back and it would take a while for them to get settled back in. Not that they were drunk, but they'd had maybe a drink before dinner and a glass of wine and so forth, and they'd be a little bit late getting back. What I tried to advocate, and I don't know what they do now, was that rather than break and come back, we should stay until six or seven or seven-thirty and go home. It also eliminated that opportunity for people to drink.

Tell us about the way the Capitol was laid out at the time. You mentioned that most of the offices were really concentrated on a couple floors. But were there other areas where people could gather and discuss things? I know a lot of people didn't even have offices.

On the third floor off the chambers you had Appropriations or Ways and Means. That was the corner office. Then you had the Transportation Committee. You had Judiciary Committee and I think that was primarily the three committee rooms on that ground floor. I may be leaving out something but I don't think so. And then on the fourth floor you had very small committee rooms that would hold the members. There may be some still up there like that.

On the Senate side, where the Senate attorneys are office'd on the fourth floor, that was one of the original committee rooms. So you probably had eight or 10 or 12 committee rooms on that fourth floor, all virtually the same size. You couldn't get more than six or eight people in those offices. Also, on the third floor you had a post office and the sergeant-at-arms' office and a page room. They were all combined. Then you had the men's lounge and the ladies' lounge. I think they're used for caucusing now. Of course you had the speaker's office. That was it. So you didn't have any place to go.

I think I mentioned that they had two WATS lines to handle all the long-distance calls that went out. Can you imagine that today? So the only place members had to go to visit is on the floor. Most members came back at night. Correspondence was very minor. They did have what they called the steno pool that was housed down on the first floor. And I think for the Senate they had about 15 or 17 stenographers. If you were a member and wanted to answer some letters, you would call the steno supervisor and she would put you on the list and arrange a time. She would send a person up who would sit in the chair next to the member's chair and the member would dictate letters. You'd get back the typed letter within a few days, depending on the load she had. If you were fortunate enough to be a committee chair in those offices upstairs, you had a desk in the corner. So maybe they had two desks in there for committee chairs.

I saw an article mentioning that there was a lot of patronage. I think it was the sergeant-at-arms, Charlie Johnson, who at that time had five family members on his payroll. The article appeared to be an exposé on how Olympia was paying for everybody and their brother to work down there during the session. How accurate was that?

One of the great things the press did for that story was they went down and got a payroll and tried to match up names. I remember one time there was a lady who worked in the members' cafeteria and her name was Snyder, so they came running to me and wanted to know if that was a relative or if I had my mother on the payroll. That was a great time for the newspapers.

There used to be an employment committee because everybody was hired for the session, or most everybody was hired for the session. People put in applications and they got people to sponsor them for the different positions. Usually the employment committee—which I helped on—would go around the table and people would say they would like to have so-and-so be a security person or a committee clerk or whatever. And then you tried to give everybody the person they'd sponsored. I guess that's the patronage system about as heavy as it gets. But also you did have to have some professionals hired. Originally, each house had its own bill drafting. They'd hire attorneys to draft bills for the session. That's before we had the setup we have today. So, it's really a lot better system today and they have a professional staff and caucus staffs. We don't ask people their party affiliations.

And yet the top offices still are political appointments.

Oh, yes.

But below that they try to make them nonpartisan?

Yes. The Senate Research Center has staff. They have a different name for it now, but the House has something similar. Those people are all hired without any political background checks. Sometimes they turn out to be Democrats or Republicans. I think occasionally there is somebody who's let go because they might have a political affiliation, but that's a rarity anymore. You see people around there who work for the Democrats. Then the Republicans take over and they work for them. It's a pretty good system now. I liked Charlie and I don't want to say anything, but he kind of operated along the edge. You know what I mean? He had a beer distributorship here in town. He was a member at one time in the House. It was kind of strange. He was a beer distributor and the other member from the 22nd District, Claude Lorimer, was a minister.

That's interesting!

That's when members of the House didn't run by position. You voted for two and you could vote for two Democrats, two Republicans, or one of each. Something went wrong with the forklift at Charlie's beer distributorship and he borrowed one from the state, which was right next door to him. That got him in trouble. It was just kind of poor judgment— poor judgment things that he would do. And then it was customary that if you got your first bill passed you treated the other members to something. It used to be cigars for the men and candy for the ladies. And the members would go to Charlie and he'd buy the cigars or he'd have already bought them and the candy and there was always speculation that Charlie made a profit on the members like that.

In the House, for example, you have the chief clerk. Is there usually only one assistant? Tell me a little bit about how the whole office was organized.

Normally, except for 1963 when Gene Prince and I shared the job, there's one assistant chief clerk and a secretary to the chief clerk.

The duties of that position were primarily secretarial?

Right, even though Si Holcomb gave Marie Davis and Lucille Rohrbeck a little extra power, I would say. They had things to do that normally a secretary wouldn't have. Like in the Senate, Ward Bowden had Florence Kenderesi. When I went over to the Senate I kept her on until she retired. Like I say, in those years it was starting to change where there were people working the year-round. I think with Florence, she would work fulltime until Dorothy Greeley, who was our *Journal* clerk, finished with her chore of getting the *Journal* out, and then I think they split the job so somebody would be in the office. And then the caucus added an employee in I think '71.

So there would be three people in the chief clerk's office?

Yes. And when the session came along they usually hired an additional person in the office to answer the telephone and act as a backup.

Beyond that sort of nuclear office, then the chief clerk would also be in charge of the bill room?

Yes. We hired for the positions. Seems like we always would save a spot or two because somebody would come in and say his neighbor lost his job and has two or three kids, can you get him a job as security or something like that? So we always saved a couple or three spots for emergency purposes.

The 1965 session was the year where the Art Commission came in. And talk about putting murals in the Legislative Building began. Of course, later that became a huge issue when the murals proved controversial. Do you remember how that all got started?

We had a committee. I know Senator Walter Williams from King County was very involved in doing something. But that was a controversy that has been there as long as the building has. Have you ever heard of Ken Callahan?

Yes. The Northwest artist?

Yes. Well, Ken Callahan—I should call him Kenneth—lived two blocks from us in Long Beach for years. One time—and this was back in the 1930s—he entered a state contest for a mural design. Different artists came into the Capitol and said what they would put in. Probably all of the ideas, or Ken Callahan's at least, ended up in archives. One time, Ralph Munro, the secretary of state, dug them out and had them on display in his office. He invited Ken up to show the drawings and how they would fit in different places in the building. The drawings are still around and they've got to be worth some money, too, I would think. Well, Ken said, "I don't like them." I guess that's a typical artist.

He didn't like his own old work?

"Don't like them!" he said. But anyhow they were of covered wagons and early logging and things like that.

What ways did the approach to the speakership differ between Bob Schaefer and Don Eldridge when Eldridge took over in 1967? Did they have different philosophies or ways of approaching that office?

I don't think there was a lot of difference except I think maybe Schaefer had a little more of an open office. He tried to give everybody a chance to come in and see him that wanted to. And I think Don's office was maybe a little tighter. He didn't let everybody in. Maybe that's the best way to run it because a lot of people will come in wasting your time, and time for the speaker is extremely valuable.

In reading Don Eldridge's discussion of his term as speaker, he said he was a little more laissez-faire. I think his motto was "let 'em talk." Does the speaker determine the length and breadth of the discussion that takes place on the floor? Do they really shape that?

That's kind of hard to say. I think a lot depends on what stage of the session they're in, how much work they have left to do, and how much work they want to get accomplished before the session is over. Sometimes you might want to let debate drag on. If you have the speakership you can always demand the previous question and cut off debate. I know one thing: In the Senate when I was the majority leader, I didn't invoke the three-minute rule—that you can only talk three minutes and you can only talk once. The reason I didn't like it is you can cut off debate by demanding the previous question. When you had a three-minute rule and you could only speak once, that's at the end of the session when your most important bills are going through, and sometimes to cut somebody out of speaking twice is a big disservice to the whole process. Maybe we did on the very last day or something, but I don't think I ever imposed that three-minute rule.

So it's really feeling out the situation and what kind of action is required?

Yes. And there's not as much debate anymore. There is sometimes on certain bills, but if you roll out the budget sometimes the debate would take three or four hours. In the 1980s when they were struggling to balance the budget, sometimes the House would go all night under Dan Grimm as the Ways and Means chairman. Grimm didn't encourage the debates; he was just subjected to them. But they'd start at seven o'clock and end at five in the morning. Now, when I was there, on the budget, they had things pretty well ironed out and they'd gone through the amendment process in committee and the minority party would offer some of the amendments again on the floor, but they would have just specific ones that they wanted to get a recorded vote on. Then give one or two speeches on each side, sometimes not that many. Used to be the budget was out there on final passage and almost everybody spoke on it. So, I don't think it's as important to have that three-minute rule. I don't know if people realize that those things aren't as important as they once thought they were.

We had been talking earlier about the Republicans coming in and gaining control in the mid-1960s. Not only do you have Schaefer, then Eldridge, as speakers, but by 1967 you also have Slade Gorton as majority leader, coming out with a lot of proposed rule changes. There was the reduction of the number of committees. There also was Rule 38, that a motion to postpone indefinitely can be made at any time except during the first reading. Evidently, there'd been abuses in the House where people moved to postpone even during the first readings, so the bill never got a hearing at all.

I think that really goes back to the 1947 session when the Republicans took over control and used that rule a lot. Anyhow, in the 1960s they were discussing this rule change—if it wasn't indefinitely postponed it was something else, but I think it was indefinitely postponed. Slim Rasmussen, the Democrat from Tacoma who was first elected to the Legislature in 1944, was still around in the 1970s, and they were still talking about the rule. And Slim said, "I can remember when the Republicans pulled that on us 150-some times, and I don't think we should eliminate that rule." I remember I kind of piped up and said, "If I may say a word, I think Senator Rasmussen is referring to the 1947 session in the House of Representatives," which he was. I think Senator Phil Talmadge and someone else who was about Talmadge's age looked at one another. "We weren't even born yet," they said.

There was another one about ranking of motions where a motion to lay an amendment on the table could not carry the main question with it unless so specified in the motion to table.

Yes. Essentially saying that if the amendment went, the bill was dead, too.

OK. And that was common up to that point?

Not that common. But you had to be a little careful if you were going to put an amendment up because it might kill your bill. On the other hand, if you wanted to kill the bill, you put the amendment up and it would fail. Like I say, today there's none of that type of parliamentary maneuvering like they had in the old days.

So Gorton was aware of all these sort of small issues?

Oh, sure. Oh, sure. He was a master at that.

One of the rules essentially had a clause that said no standing committee shall vote on an issue by secret ballot. And then there was a big debate about whether that applied to the Rules Committee. At least up to that point it had always been secret.

They still had secret votes in the Rules Committee because it was after I went over to the Senate that it was changed. And the Rules Committee's votes were closed-door, too. They'd have executive sessions where they'd go in and vote. Of course the big thing was that if you wanted to kill a bill, you killed it in the Senate Rules Committee. Hundreds of bills would die in Senate Rules because they had the secret ballot. Members could promise to vote for a bill and go in and nobody would know the difference.

When Republicans were in power and you were still assistant chief clerk of the House, would you go into Republican caucuses?

Oh, no. I never went in.

When you were assistant chief clerk and the Democrats were in power, would you have gone in and collected ballots if Si Holcomb wasn't around?

Yes. I usually went. And I think that started in 1957 when Si wasn't there. When he came back, the members still wanted me in there, if I remember correctly.

What did you find most interesting or compelling about the assistant chief clerk's job? What was it that brought you back year after year even though you had another livelihood?

I think the uniqueness of it was probably the big thing. Some people may enjoy mountain climbing or some other sport or other endeavor. You can work in a grocery store or have a grocery store lots of places. Be a banker or be a logger or whatever, but there's only one Legislature and that's where the action is. That's where decisions are made that affect everybody in the state one way or another. You meet a lot of interesting people. People who most likely are going to run for the Legislature are not weak-kneed; they're strong personalities, and it's enjoyable to be around people like that.

We talked about the new Republican majority in 1967. With all those new members, most of whom hadn't been in the Legislature before, does that put more pressure on you as staff?

Probably a little bit. A member comes in new and who are they going to turn to? They're going to turn to the senior members. They're going to turn to staff, of which there weren't too many around, so I think that's why Si Holcomb held forth for so many years because he was an adviser to the members and newcomers. Of course we had new speakers practically every two years back in the '30s and '40s. They needed help and Si was the one who was there to give them help.

Did each speaker have a different style, or were they molded more by their party?

A speaker might have a different program. Why do people run for the Legislature? In most cases, if they've been a school board member, they're interested in education. If that person happens to end up as speaker their program is probably going to be education. I think Bill Day got involved because he had a daughter who had a disability. I'm quite sure he lobbied before he ran for the Legislature. But, a lot of people get interested because they have one particular subject that they're interested in. So, sure, people have different backgrounds. They're going to be more interested in things they've been involved with in their private life.

Were there some characteristics that seemed to be imperative to succeed in the speakership?

No. I think the speakers always kind of rose to the occasion. What makes a good speaker is to be able to get in and get out of the session and pass a budget. That's the main reason you're there. And in order to do that, you have to have lots of little coalitions within your own party and you have to reach across the aisle occasionally to come up with some votes. One of the most eloquent things I heard in my half century at the Capitol was Governor Dan Evans' declaration in his 1972 inaugural address that he would "rather cross the aisle than cross the people."

I wanted to ask you about another issue that came up in both 1967 and 1969—the California wine bill. I know that one of the advocates of the bill to reduce restrictions on sales of California wines was Representative Hal Wolf, a Republican who was in the grocery business. In your position as assistant chief clerk of the House or secretary of the Senate, would you follow bills more closely if they affected your personal life?

Oh yes, I kept tabs on the wine bill. And the Grocers Association lobbied hard for it. In fact, I just came across a letter from a fellow who was lobbying for it. "Big Mac" McGowan was the executive director of the Food Dealers' Association. But the main lobbyist wasn't the Grocers Association. It was a lobbyist named Tom Owens, whose nickname was "Tommy Raincoat." Tom lobbied for the bill, and I think he's the one that did the real work. I remember he came to the beach and I made a reservation for a place for him to stay and to go fishing. And he had, what's the winery from California, the big one?

Gallo?

Yes, he had one of the Gallos with him on the fishing trip. Most of Washington's wines at that time were fortified wines. Washington grape growers were opposed to the wine bill because it ended their preferential treatment. But it turned out to be the best thing that ever happened to them because they started growing different kinds of grapes and producing world-class wines. The Washington wine business is now just amazing. But, yes, the wine bill was a big bill.

There were lots of charges on both sides, but particularly against the lobbyists for the California wine industry—that they were spreading around way too much money and using hard-pressure tactics. Is that something that you saw?

I knew those accusations were going on. But all the years I was around there, I never saw any money change hands. I never saw and was never offered anything to pull a bill or anything like that. I can't say that there wasn't any, but I certainly wasn't privy to anything like that.

I know one time I got criticized. I think I had $600 in so-called gifts. Well, one of them was when I had gone to a football game at the University of Washington. For years, they invited legislators to football games. So it was reported as a gift to me, for $80 or whatever it was for the lunch and the tickets. From then on when I got invited I wrote a check for that amount.

Another thing that was reported as a gift was when there was some kind of meeting up at Hood Canal. A lobbyist for the oil industry invited me to speak at a breakfast. There were three other legislators there, one from each of the four caucuses. I got there a little late, and they had a condo for me and then a buffet-type breakfast. I participated in this forum and by 9:30 I was back on the road. And I got a letter from somebody giving me hell for accepting all these gifts [the room and meal]. I wrote back and said, "I paid my own mileage and my own car, and I didn't bill them for that. The irony was that this was Senate business. I could have billed the Senate for my room and meals and mileage there and back." But it came out in the paper as a gift. So I wrote a check for it. The only bad thing about that is other people might not be in a position to write a check. There's a few that live on their legislative salary and maybe their spouse works.

We were invited to go to a Rose Bowl game, the leadership was, and we flew down with the team and other dignitaries. But I paid for everything. And I had to hound the University of Washington to find out how much the airfare was. But I reimbursed them for the room and everything else. And there was an article about all the legislators going down. The last sentence said, "Sid Snyder reimbursed the university for his pass to the Rose Bowl." So when I did anything I reimbursed. And that's a hell of a note because I could afford to reimburse. For the other members, this may be their only income. I kind of got off on a tangent here. But I think there's a lot of members now that reimburse because they don't want to be in the papers that make them look like they're doing all these free things that the commoner doesn't get to do. The governor was also on the plane to the Rose Bowl. Dino Rossi was, too. And Speaker Clyde Ballard was there with his wife.

Did different sessions vary in terms of camaraderie and how people got along party lines?

Yes. But it always isn't Democrats and Republicans. Sometimes it's the country mice versus the city mice. And there are fewer country mice today than there are city mice.

What was the relationship between the legislators and the staff?

I think most members were very appreciative of the staff because most everybody worked hard and long hours.

What about socially, especially when you were either assistant chief clerk or secretary of the Senate?

I was included with members a lot of times, and it was very customary for lobbyists to take members out every night for dinner. Members would look for somebody to take them out to dinner. This was back when the pay and the per diem weren't as good. I remember one incident at the Elks Club. We'd worked till probably 11 o'clock. So we went down and Al Rosellini was there. And the governor ended up at our table. They announced the last call for alcohol and he said, "Well, I better call my driver." And we said, "We'll drop you off." I think there were two carloads of us, probably seven or eight people. And he said, "Well that's fine but you'll have to come in and have a drink." So we pull up to the mansion at one o'clock. We go in and the governor of the State of Washington pours us all a drink.

Did you sometimes get frustrated, especially as a senator, with the media?

I get disgusted with the press occasionally because of their criticism. "Well, the Legislature has been there for so many days and they have only gotten two bills to the governor's office..." I don't think you want legislators going to Olympia and shoving a lot of bills down to the governor's office before you've had hearings in both houses; before you've had votes in both houses; before you've had people come in and testify. I know I've thought bills at first were of great value and when it came time to vote it turned out that I was opposed to them.

I'll give you one example: There was a bill to prohibit telephone solicitations. I thought, "Gee, that's a wonderful idea." They had a hearing on the bill, and come to find out there were several hundred people in the state or maybe even a few thousand who were handicapped and made their living selling on the telephone. Well, that's a whole different story, so I changed my mind about whether I would support that bill. Do you want to take their livelihoods away? Do you want to take the self-assurance they have by providing their own livelihoods? No, you don't. So you want the process to work, and it does work.

Sometimes the press would say the bills that were passed were "nothing" bills. I'll give you another example: There's a place called Puget Island in Wahkiakum County. Right across the bridge from Puget Island there's a Norse Hall that's been there for years and has seen tough times. They have 25 or 30 members and they're lucky to save enough money to put a new roof on every 25 years. They had rented the building to a lady who gave dance lessons. Come to find out, they can't rent it for a commercial purpose, and that's considered a commercial purpose. If they do, they lose their property-tax exemption. So the county auditor came, a lady that I've known. In fact, her former husband was Don Talley, a state senator. She said, "Can you do anything for us?" So we dropped a bill in that said if they rented it for the use for the arts—dancing would be an art—they could rent it and not lose their tax exemption. Of course you can't do something that is only good for Wahkiakum County. And you didn't want it to be good for all the counties in the state. So we put a section in the bill that said this only applies to counties with a population of less than 10,000. That covered Wahkiakum County and about two or three other counties. Those people were ecstatic with that bill. It probably cost the state maybe $200 or $300 a year in tax money. Those are the "nothing" bills that passed. I think those people deserve representation, just like Boeing or Weyerhaeuser or anybody else. It gets a little sickening when we don't get good coverage from the press. But I guess that wouldn't make interesting reading.

But you have used the press to your benefit, too.

I pushed the gas tax before one passed and wrote guest editorials for it and so forth. I pointed out how much it's needed and how much slowing down traffic costs businesses. I can't remember now the name of the radiator-repair business in Seattle, but they were having trouble because they couldn't get parts from one of their stores to another because traffic was so bad. But Grays Harbor gets a rolling two dollars for every dollar they've paid in gas tax. Cowlitz I think is about the same. Maybe a little less. Pacific I think gets four or five times what they paid in. Wahkiakum County was eight times, I think. So I had an editorial in the Longview paper or the *Wahkiakum County Eagle*. Some guy wrote and said, "Aren't you going to fight to keep it that way?" So I did write back and say, "King, Snohomish, and Pierce counties have all or part of 29 of the 49 legislative districts. What if they said, 'Hey, let's just give them back what they put in?' You wouldn't be riding the ferry from Cathlamet over to Oregon for 40 or 50 people working from Wahkiakum County. You'd have to drive around." I never heard from the guy again. There was a little more to it than that. And Pierce County just built a new Narrows Bridge with help from the gas tax.

The toll keeps going up, too.

But you know what, I think when I was in the Senate, Pierce County had paid in $500 million more than they'd received back over the previous 10 years. So they do have something to complain about.

What was your take on the time in 1969 when the Black Panthers came down to Olympia?

I remember they were standing out there with guns and we had the doors barred. They had a log or something big pounding on the door trying to get in. We were very, very nervous, because we didn't know what was going to happen. I remember Senator Martin Durkan was standing inside the door when they were pounding. He asked the State Patrol, "Do you want to open up and let some of them in?" I bet the troopers actually said "No." We didn't know what would happen, if they would overrun it. But there were some Black Panthers standing outside like they were guarding the place. It turned out to be very, very peaceful. I think there was a former Black Panther running for the U.S. Senate at this time.

Was the Senate at the time you began working there any more or less partisan than the House?

Of course, they'd had coalitions in the Senate, too. In fact, I have a picture somewhere that shows some coalitionists with Al Rosellini.

When you came in as secretary of the Senate in 1969, you were the choice of a group of people, including Bill Gissberg, Augie Mardesich and Gordon Walgren. Bob Grieve, who was still majority leader, had a camp of his own. Were you stepping into a hot political situation?

Oh, I'm sure of that, because how do you take politics out of politics? You just can't do that. I can remember when Mardesich decided to take on Greive for the leadership spot. I was with Mardesich on that. Very quietly. I had lunch with Mardesich and a couple of others who were talking about this and I went along to talk about the procedures. Augie said, "Maybe you don't want to be here. Maybe you want to leave?" I said, "No, it's fine with me."

With The Evergreen State College nearby, there are always protests at the Capitol, right? There was the classic story that one of the students stood up on a desk and urinated on it.

Yeah. That was in the House, I think, when I was in the Senate. And they camped overnight in the House one night. Those were Evergreen students, too.

There were some movements at various times to get rid of the whole college.

Some of the members were very bitter about Evergreen State College. Some of the more conservative Republicans would just as soon close it down.

Some say the civil disobedience that comes from having a college such as Evergreen is a good thing on many levels.

Oh, I do too. When I retired in 2002, Governor Locke offered me a board of directors' position at Evergreen, which I turned down. Then he asked if I was interested in the same at Lower Columbia or Grays Harbor colleges, and I turned both of those down because I didn't want to choose one over the other. Although it really wouldn't have made much difference after I was out of there.

You won an award as national legislator of the year and donated the cash prize to both of the colleges—correct?

Yes. We went to Denver to receive the award. I have a nice trophy downstairs in my house. I got $10,000 to give to charity. I split it between Lower Columbia and Grays Harbor. The award was named in honor of William M. Bulger, former president of the Massachusetts State Senate. Ironically, in the last year or so Bulger's brother was one of the Ten Most Wanted fugitives.

A trip that two transportation committee members took to Europe to study the rapid transit system there in 1969 got a lot of media attention when they expensed the trip at 10 cents a mile. It led to a major change in the compensation rules. I wonder what that would be like at today's rate.

Fifty cents. Maybe even more. I remember Senators Al Henry and Gordy Walgren and others were in Japan on a transportation issue. Al Henry was a huge man, and in Japan they were all sitting with their legs crossed and singing songs. They and an interpreter, and Al Henry sang "Minnie the Mermaid." Bette and I were on some of these trips and we paid our own way. These trips were headed up by Lieutenant Governor John Cherberg. He gathered up all kinds of things for gifts. He'd start out with maybe 20 or 30 books on Washington and when he got to Taiwan, the last stop on the trip, all he had left were Mariners T-shirts. And they were stamped "Made in Taiwan."

In the mid 1970s, when Augie Mardesich was the Senate majority leader, he was accused of extorting $10,000 from two garbage company executives in exchange for voting for something that would benefit them. Did he resign after that?

No. Augie got beat. He got beat in the 1978 primary by Larry Vognild, another Democrat. What beat Augie was that he made a change in the pension system from PERS 1 to PERS 2. Because PERS 1 was and is so expensive that it was going to bankrupt us. Maybe bankrupt is the wrong word, but we've got troubles right now because of the pension system taking so much money. But Augie got that changed and it hurt the firemen and the policemen and they went out and beat him. I think at the time Augie saved the state a billion bucks. Like I said, the firemen and the policemen are good backers of Democrats. I think Augie was in Alaska fishing when the primary election came along. There were just two Democrats and Larry Vognild beat Augie.

Gordy Walgren took the Senate leadership role after Mardesich. How were those two different from each other as leaders?

There was a lot of similarity to them. Both bright guys. Both good politicians. Augie to me was the brightest Democrat I ever saw or worked with. And Slade Gorton is the brightest Republican. Yet they were different—Augie and Slade. I told you some Augie stories. He was a strong backer of teaching a second language in schools. He came from a Slav community and he said he couldn't speak a word of English when he started school. They spoke Slav at home: "If I could do it, others could do it, too."

Walgren, of course, is your good friend. He was involved in the "Gamscam" scandal. I know you always stood by his side.

The crime is that Gordon Walgren was convicted of something that he was absolutely innocent of.

After serving a stint in prison, he got his law license back?

He passed the bar again, and was readmitted to the practice of law. He lobbies in Olympia. Probably most of the members don't even know Gordon was convicted and served two years.

In your opinion, was Governor Dixy Lee Ray involved in the prosecution of Walgren and House Speaker John Bagnariol?

Yeah. I can't just sit here and explain it in a few words. You need to have the whole thing spread out. Gordon was served with a summons at a hotel near SeaTac airport. He was at a meeting. The FBI agent said, "Now, I'll take you to the courthouse and let you make your plea and you'll be out of there." As he was leaving the Courthouse, there was Ruth Walsh, a reporter from KOMO 4. Gordon thinks the U.S. attorney tipped her off.

How would you characterize Dixy's tenure as governor?

I think she was scared that everybody was after her. But the one person who went down and said, "Governor, I want to work with you" was Augie Mardesich. She appointed him to the Tax Appeals Board or something like that.

There was a 1974 incident I wanted to talk to you about. It was when Senators Al Henry and Perry Woodall accused Slade Gorton, who was then attorney general, and a *P-I* reporter by the name of Shelby Scates of improper conduct because they belonged to an investment club together. I guess the Senate had an unrecorded vote on the matter but it was never disclosed what happened. I had never heard the resolution. Do you remember that incident?

I bought Al Henry's share of the investment club, so it seems like I would remember that part of it. But it mainly consisted of Bob Twigg, who was a Republican member from Spokane. And it mainly consisted of property in Cusack. Someone bought a ranch up there because there was speculation they were going to build some kind of aluminum plant or some such thing. And there was some property in Spokane, and there was some property on a lake up in northern Washington, too. It never turned out to be a very good investment.

In Governor Ray's penultimate session, 1979, there was a split house and co-speakers. How rare was that? And were there frustrations in dealing with a House that's split like that?

Oh, yeah. There was another one, too, later on. But in 1979 it was Bagnariol and Duane Berentson. Bagnariol is a Democrat, and Berentson a Republican. They were good friends and they got along well. One of them presided one day; the other one presided the next day. Some of the committees were split. We got along fairly well that way.

It doesn't seem that would be very productive, though.

No, but we made it through. And then there was one later on with Clyde Ballard from Wenatchee and Frank Chopp from Seattle. It was the House's turn to work the budget first. And they didn't send the budget over. Didn't send the budget over. We kept waiting. And I said, "If they don't send one over, we, the Senate, will send one over by the 100th day." We sent it over on the 102nd day. And on the 105th day, which was the last day, we arranged a couple Republican votes for the budget. I think Clyde Ballard ended up in the hospital that day.

Was it typical that everyone would vote with their party? Was that pretty much the way it always worked?

There were a few times I can remember that the budget in the Senate got maybe 41 or 42 votes out of 49.

What about you when became a senator. Did you vote with your party all the time?

Yes. You couldn't have the majority leader voting against it and tell all your colleagues, "Oh you guys vote for it. I'm not going to vote for this."

Warren Magnuson was one of Snyder's favorite politicians and also one with whom others compared him favorably. He and Bette spent time with the senator in Washington, D.C. *Snyder family photo*

I'm not necessarily asking about the budget, but about all issues.

Oh, sure, I probably cast votes that I wouldn't have because you go along with the party.

A legislator resigned on the floor in 1980 after being charged with lewd conduct with a couple of men in a public restroom in Olympia. He maintained he was innocent and not a homosexual.

One of the Olympia Brewery people was involved.

The lawmaker was pressured to resign, of course. It was a different time. We now have openly gay politicians across the country and it isn't that big a deal.

We've got several in the Legislature.

Snyder visits with longtime Lieutenant Governor John Cherberg
in Cherberg's office in the mid-1980s. *Louie Balukoff*

The same year, Mount St. Helens erupted.

I think it helped beat Warren Magnuson. He flew out here with Jimmy
Carter to see the impact. I can remember him getting off Air Force One
and looking very old. And I think that helped Slade Gorton beat him.
Maggie looked old and feeble when he got off the plane.

**Tell me about working with John Cherberg? Here was an old football
player and coach from UW. Did he have that gruff personality that
you think of a football player having?**

Very opposite. He was a gentleman.

Was he a big man?

No. I doubt if he was six feet tall. Probably weighed 175. He was a star
in the 1930s. I can remember when they had 200-pound linemen and
that was huge. Now they're 330, you know, six-five and so forth. But

Cherberg was a running back. And later a coach at the UW. He got fired. And he was very bitter about that forever. Like I said, he was a gentleman and his office was almost always open. If I had somebody in town visiting I could always take them in to meet Cherberg. And they would leave and say, "Oh my, he's the nicest guy in the world." And he was. Very gracious. I remember one time that Bette and I and her dad were in Olympia for some reason, out of session. I probably was the assistant chief clerk in the House. We were having lunch at the Tyee and Cherberg was in there. He walked by our table with Ward Bowden, who was secretary of the Senate at the time. And they stopped and visited and Bette's dad was so impressed he would always ask, "How's that fellow Cherberg doing?" Because he made such an impression on people. And he was a good parliamentarian. He learned that from scratch, probably with Ward Bowden as his teacher. But he could hold grudges. His wife, Betty, was a great person, a good politician's wife. I even knew him not to go to functions that he was invited to if she wasn't invited. They came to visit us in Long Beach regularly.

Several Seahawk and Sonic players came down, too. Including Steve Largent, who stepped over into the political world after his playing days were over. From what you knew of him did you see him as a politician?

I'm not surprised. We still hear from him at Christmas. I don't know how many years he came down, two or three or four different years. It was kind of a ritual.

Were they all good guys?

Oh, yeah. Jim Zorn, on his Christmas cards, he always has a quote from the Bible. Largent would sit there and watch the other team on *Monday Night Football* and he'd say, "Gosh, he's a nice guy. He's a good player." I mean I never heard him say anything bad about anyone.

Snyder met his share of powerful dignitaries over the years, including several presidents. Here he, Bette, and grandson Cole Paxton, meet with President Bill Clinton. *Snyder family photo*

Sid and Bette met Al Gore when he was vice president and also when he was campaigning for president in 2000. *Snyder family photo*

Did anyone else of note visit you over the years at Long Beach? Did you run into celebrities at the store?

This is a lot of years ago. Sid, our son, was 15 and he's 60 now. But when they had the Ocean Shores Classic golf tournament they invited all these celebrities to it. They had a great list of celebrities. One night I was working at the store. Bette was working. Young Sid was working. That was a typical June. A couple guys walked in and one of them came over to me and said, "My friend walked over to get some beer and I want to be sure and pay for it." And he handed me $20 and I thought, "God sakes, I've seen that fellow before. In Olympia? Did I go to school with him?" All of a sudden I said, "Are you Dizzy Dean?" And he drawled, "That's right, partner." I called young Sid up to the front. He was stocking shelves, and he just turned red. And Bette said, "What are you doing in town, Dizzy?" "Well," he said, "I'm going to try to catch one of those-there sal-mon." And Bette said, "You'll never want to go pigeon hunting down in Wiggins again." Dizzy used to always talk about pigeon hunting in Wiggins, Mississippi. Young Sid got a baseball off the toy rack and had him sign it. He's still got it. Should have had him sign a dozen of them.

Wonder what those would be worth today.

Yeah! Anyhow, Dizzy was headed up to the Classic and he had a friend in Longview or Kelso that he was staying with and they came here to fish. The Longview paper sent a reporter up to cover him. By this time, word had spread that Dizzy was in town. He was in the store two or three more times after that. The reporter talked about how Dizzy was gracious with everybody down at the dock waiting for him. And I think the last sentence of the article was, "He acted like he didn't realize the celebrity that he really is."

I think that last sentence describes you as well, especially in Long Beach.

I just feel I'm Sid Snyder, and I'm not any better than anybody else and nobody else is any better than I am.

Ever get a feeling that you don't want to go out in public some days because you don't want to have to talk to people?

Oh, no.

You're appreciative of the fact that people do want to talk to you?

Well, yeah, *if* they want to talk to me. Especially when I was a member, that was part of my job. I tried to get around the district a lot and go to meetings.

The 19th District spans such a large area. You must have put several thousand miles on your cars over the years.

I rarely, if ever, turned down an invite to go somewhere. Only if there was a conflict. On rare occasions I might have, hypothetically, a luncheon in Longview and an evening meeting in Aberdeen. So I would leave Long Beach in the morning, drive to Longview, leave Longview, drive to Aberdeen, then drive home. It was 240 miles. I used to put up to 30,000 a year on my car. And then you have to consider that when we were in session it was just one trip a week.

But if you were in Seattle…

Yes, 15 minutes and you've covered your district.

Did you come home on the weekends?

I always did. When we had a weekend session I might not get home, but that was very rare.

You thought it was important to attend every event you could.

Well, yeah, I was elected and I had that duty. I used to often say, "Well, when I was home on the weekend and back in the real world…" I would talk to people in the store, and people would talk to me. And you'd be surprised by the people who would come up to you and start talking about an issue in the Legislature. You really got some grassroots feelings being at home, being around the local community.

That's another aspect of being in a rural area you wouldn't find in a big city: accessibility. People knew where to find you. Did you take a lot of grief at times?

Not a lot. And I had a reputation, "You've got a problem, call Sid's office."

Tell me about the time you tricked Bob Basich, the lawmaker from Aberdeen who coached at Grays Harbor College.

In one of the redistrictings in the early 1980s, the 19th District was split into an A and a B district. They took half of the district—part of Grays Harbor, part of Pacific and part of Wahkiakum—and that became 19-B. Then they took the rest of it, which was most of Cowlitz and the remainder of Wahkiakum, and that was 19-A. The Senate passed a bill in 1990 that eliminated the split so it would be just like all the other districts in the state. I was still secretary of the Senate. The Republicans wouldn't vote for it because there was a fellow by the name of Bobby Williams who was their representative from the Cowlitz district. And if they eliminated that line Bobby would have to run in Pacific and Grays Harbor, which are heavier Democrat, and he probably wouldn't get re-elected. Well, the bill to end the split got over to the House and Basich put his foot on it. He didn't want to be running in the combined district.

So there was a one-day special session that had something to do with Hanford. It was also the last day of filing. Basich had filed and nobody had filed against him. Denny Heck was chief clerk. He and I got together and said it's a shame that Basich is going to get a free ride because he's costing

Snyder and fellow Democratic legislators Bob Basich, center, and Brad Owen, discuss an issue in the mid-1990s. Kathy Quigg, *The Daily World*

the Democrats a member. So I said, "Denny, why don't you put my name [on a filing report] as running against Basich? And just have it on one copy and be sure he gets that one." I didn't know if I could beat him or not. Then Denny called and said, "Sid, you better get over here! Basich is really upset. He's got that one copy and he's going around pointing to your name on there." So I walked across the hall and walked up on the House rostrum and here comes Basich. "Sid, I didn't think you'd do that to me!" I said, "I wanted to run for the Legislature, but I can't because of that damn line in there." It went on like that for a while. Finally Denny said, "You better save that copy Bob, that's the only one with Sid's name on it."

"What?!" Basich exclaimed.

"That's the only one with Sid's name on it. Sid hasn't filed."

"Oh, you sons of bitches!" He put his arms around both of us and kind of collapsed.

In fact, I brought a lawsuit that the splitting of the 19th was unconstitutional because I only got to vote for one of the two representatives. But the Supreme Court ruled 7-to-2 against me. People thought it was purely political. It was a big part political, but it was also, "Hey, I'm not being treated fairly."

How much is involved in bringing up a lawsuit like that?

I hired Jeff Campiche, a former Pacific County prosecutor. It cost me a couple thousand dollars. We had some other names on it. Fred Dore voted with me and I can't remember who else did.

It was just a matter of principle for you doing that—right? You didn't stand to gain anything.

Yeah. The other 47 districts all had two members—two positions they could vote for. Redistricting now is done by commission.

How much studying of the bills did you do when you were a senator before you voted on them?

Well, most of it's done for you. Especially if you're on, say, the Education Committee. If you're on the committee you've heard all the testimony on the bill, all the pros and cons there are. Then we go to caucus. In the caucus you go down all the bills on the calendar and get an explanation. So you're pretty well versed on everything that gets to the floor.

You're on record as saying you never accepted any favors in exchange for your vote.

No. And I don't think anybody really has. It gets so disgusting.

Were there ever any issues you can recall where your constituency was split down the middle? Because the 19th is so large. How did you reconcile those when they came to pass?

You just make a decision: This is it. I don't know that there were that many issues that were that divisive because there is a lot of similarity with logging and ports and so forth. Most of the time the district was on the same page. But we took the time. I always paid attention to the little guy that never thought he could get the ear of a legislator. But I was also interested in legislation that Weyerhaeuser and the biggies in the district were interested in. In my mind they were usually equal. It wasn't too many years ago that we were giving all kinds of tax credits and so forth. Give a tax credit to Longview Fiber Company and that means jobs. I had some neighbors call me one time. The husband worked outside of the home and the wife had a little nursery business. He worked there too. And it was going along quite well. They both worked evenings and

Snyder and Republican Senator Jack Metcalf listen to Greg Sorlie of the Department of Ecology talk about the health effects of the Weyerhaeuser settling ponds in Aberdeen in 1991. Metcalf, of Whidbey Island, was elected to Congress in 1994.
Brian DalBalcon, *The Daily World*

weekends. They raised trees that grew well along riverbanks and sold them to help fight erosion and so forth. They needed to expand and build. And they went in to get their permit and it was fine until they were asked, "Where's your architectural drawing?" They called me, explained what happened. I dropped a bill and got it through. I called them up to Olympia and we got our picture taken with the governor signing the bill. Makes me feel really good. Of course, the architects showed up to testify against it.

They want the work.

Yeah. But it was kind of ridiculous. Another classic story like that happened in the first year I was a member of the Senate. The Republicans had control. And Nabiel Shawa, who used to be city manager of Long Beach and was born and raised there, called and said, "Sid, we're having an audit and we're having a problem because we're using the hotel-motel tax money for all kinds of things. And now they're saying the only thing we can use that money for is advertising and brochures. We've been using it to pay off bonds for the boardwalk and for all kinds of things." It was getting late in the session and about deadline time for getting bills out of committee, and this hadn't even been introduced. So I got a bill and got it referred to Bob McCaslin's committee. Bob was a Republican from Spokane who I got along with real well when I was secretary of the Senate. So he moved it out of committee on an early calendar. And I got it out of Rules and onto the floor calendar, got it passed, got it to the House. We got the bill through, got it passed. And then when the next session came along we got Ilwaco included.

Then there were other bills that followed. Cowlitz County came to me, or the City of Kelso, and they had accumulated money from their hotel-motel tax. And they were restricted because the only thing they could do, according to the auditor, was use the tax for advertising in brochures. So we passed a bill that said any county—or was it the city?— that "bordered on the

Columbia River and had a national volcanic monument within the boundaries …" was included. Anyhow, we had a lot of fun over time with that.

Did you think in terms of votes when you made a decision, or did that never cross your mind?

Well, with bills like that we never had any problem.

Not those bills necessarily, but just the way you behaved. Did you ever make any decisions based on, "If I vote for this bill I'm going to lose votes in the next election"? Anything like that?

Ray Moore, an old-timer, used to say, "If you can't explain a vote you don't deserve to be there." So, no, I never worried about it.

You just worried about the people you were serving?

Yeah, that's basically it. That leads into another little story. Fishing went bad and the Port of Ilwaco didn't have enough money to put in the reserves necessary to meet the covenants of its bond plan. They say you have to pay off so much. The Port of Ilwaco was about to default. And if it had it would have driven the rates up higher for other things like water districts, sewer districts, cities, towns, and counties. I wasn't a member at the time but I got involved. A fellow by the name of Pat Dunn, who is a good friend of ours, was on Governor Spellman's staff at the time. Spellman told him, "Whatever happens, don't let the Port of Ilwaco default." At that time, you could loan money to a city and a county, and give grants, but you couldn't loan money to ports. I think it was Pat and I that came up with the idea to loan the money to the City of Ilwaco, and they in turn could loan the money to the Port of Ilwaco. And that got us over that crisis there.

I believe you were behind Referendum 48, the 1995 property-rights initiative that failed. So what was it that you liked about that referendum?

Well I didn't like the idea of the government coming in and being able to take your property. It was more of a conservative view than a liberal view.

Why do you believe it failed?

Because there were too few rural people and too many city people. [Snyder chuckled.]

That was one of the things that I wanted to talk to you about. The further east you go the more Republican you get in our state.

I think when you say "east" or "west" you should instead say "city mice" or the "country mice." That's the way I used to talk about it. Lots of times our thinking in Southwest Washington is a little closer to Eastern Washington than other parts of Western Washington. I don't think we're as conservative overall, but on certain issues I think we were. I consider myself pretty moderate, but Seattle Democrats, a lot of them thought I was a conservative.

Did the issue of splitting Washington into two states ever gain any traction in the Legislature?

No. When I was majority leader I did have a bill hearing on it or something like that. That was kind of a courtesy thing. I knew it wasn't going to pass.

Do you remember who sponsored that?

Bob McCaslin was one.

He was serious?

Oh, yeah. Probably, if you could get Oregon to go along with it. That was one idea—to combine Eastern Washington and Eastern Oregon.

It's kind of like consolidating Aberdeen, Hoquiam and Cosmopolis.

Longview and Kelso are the same.

Snyder and Democrat Lynn Kessler of Hoquiam, who served in the House from 1992-2010, were two of the most powerful legislators in the country for several years. They were the only two legislators from Washington to have received the Excellence in State Legislative Leadership Award, given annually by the National Conference of State Legislatures to the best state legislator in the country. Snyder won the award in 2002; Kessler in 2010. Kathy Quigg, *The Daily World*

Have they ever talked about consolidation?

Oh, yes!

But it's never happened. Just the whole, "I'm a Longview guy and you're a Kelso guy and we don't get along" thing?

Yeah.

If you hadn't come back after your 1997 resignation, what would the process of filling your seat have been?

There's a Constitutional provision. The precinct committeemen in the 19th District would get together and select three names. They would submit those to the commissioners of Pacific, Grays Harbor, Wahkiakum and Cowlitz counties. Those 12 commissioners would select somebody to take my place. And when I did resign for real with two years left on my term they approved Mark Doumit to take my place. And the same thing when Mark had to resign his House seat. It was a surprise when they selected the present House member from Aberdeen, Brian Blake. But he's still there. I thought a fellow from Longview would get the appointment, but he didn't. I think the Wahkiakum County commissioners and Pacific County commissioners all voted for Blake. So he was appointed.

He's been a good legislator.

I think he represents that district. Mark Doumit only served for a short time until he resigned because he couldn't afford to be a senator. Mark was a great senator. They just didn't come any better. In fact, I had members come to me and say, "What are we going to do for a new leader?" I suggested Mark but they didn't go for that. It was either going to be Lisa Brown or Harriet Spanel. And it was Lisa, and she has been the Democratic leader since.

What makes a good legislator? What separated somebody like Mark Doumit from an Average Joe?

Well, I think that anybody can talk to him. That might not sound like much but he'd been a Wahkiakum County commissioner and a House member. He had a business background too, and a college degree. He was a farmer and a fisherman in Alaska—a regular guy who could understand your problems, could sympathize with your problems. Maybe he couldn't always vote with what you wanted but he wasn't going to go out and hammer you and be so strict along party lines that you wouldn't have any flexibility. I'm proud to be a Democrat. I don't agree with everything on the Democratic platform.

You voted across the aisle?

On occasion, sure. It has to be kind of an amazing reason. Probably 95 percent of the bills that go through pass with five or less dissenting votes.

Everyone had to have a moment when they chose a party to associate with.

Everybody was a Democrat when I grew up in the 1930s.

You were a Democrat probably before you even knew what being a Democrat meant.

Yeah.

Was there any time you considered the other side?

No.

What does being a Democrat mean to you?

To me it means being progressive, treating people like you like to be treated.

Did you ever vote for a Republican?

I voted for some Republicans, but very few. Most were statewide offices.

Hypothetically, the treasurer or the auditor. They don't make policy or set policy. Dick Marquardt has been a good friend of mine and I voted for him two or three times for insurance commissioner because it is administrative. There is some policy, yes, but it isn't like being a legislator.

If you could conduct your 1997 resignation all over again would you do it the same way? Was it a matter of principle over Republicans changing the rules?

I guess I was trying to make a point. I think I would have done the same thing because there were other methods that the Republicans could have used to put a new budget up there. One story flips to mind when I mention Harriet Spanel from Bellingham. It includes Valoria Loveland from the Tri-Cities. We, the Democrats, had been in the minority and we gained control. So usually the weekend after the election we have an organizational caucus. By this point, I was Democratic leader, and had no trouble getting re-elected. But you have this organizational caucus where you elect caucus chair, majority leader, and try to line up the committee on committees to fill in who is going to be on what committees, which is usually pretty easy except when you get down to the last few people. So Harriet had been the minority leader of the Ways and Means Committee. So when we took over it would be normal that Harriet would move up and be chairman. But Valoria had been caucus chair for the Democrats and she wanted the job. Well, the committee makes all the decisions except when they get to the tough ones. Then they say, "Sid, this is your decision."

And your decision was?

Well, Valoria happened to ride with me that day from Olympia to Bellingham, or maybe it was to Seattle. We never talked one word about her being chair. But when I got there I started buttonholing members and telling them I wanted Valoria to be Ways and Means chairman. Then I want Harriet to be caucus chairman. And Harriet was really upset with

me. Some members were upset with me. I thought they just fit better with
the roles that I had chosen for them. Two or three weeks into the session,
Harriet came to me and said, "Sid, I apologize. You made the right decision." Which I guess vindicated my decision. I don't know how many members can even recall that incident now. That at least made me feel good.

Are they still in the Legislature?

No, they're both gone. Valoria was defeated, and then she ended up as
Ag Director and retired from there. Harriet ran another time and was
re-elected and then by that time she was in her early or mid-60s and she
had lost her husband, and she had had enough. It's pretty easy to have
enough around that place.

How did you stick around so long without having enough?

I talked about not running sometimes. But there are things you'd like to do.

How much did being a successful businessman have to do with you being able to stay? You just talked about Mark Doumit having to leave because financially he couldn't make ends meet, or at least not in the way he wanted to. But you didn't have that burden.

Well, I'd been around long enough. The store had grown, and I had more
employees.

How did the addition of the Astoria-Megler Bridge across the Columbia River in the 1960s affect your store in general and life on the Peninsula overall?

Well, the ferry used to quit at six or eight at night and start at six in
the morning. So it's been beneficial for both Oregon and Washington.
People go over there to shop, people work over there. So it's created
some jobs. I imagine there are some people from Oregon that work over
here, but probably not too many. But it's opened up traffic. It may not be
the perfect situation for me as a grocer but you deal with the cards you're
dealt. We have a lot of people that live here that shop over there and

that's their privilege. You get a little provoked at your fellow businessmen that shop over there—"shop locally" is what I believe in. But our competition is there. We know it and we live with it. Most of the stores are in Warrenton. Thirty minutes will get you there, 25 maybe.

Do you ever think about the whole tsunami thing that everyone is focused on nowadays?

Not that much. Sure I think about it, but if it's going to happen it might be 300 years or it might be three weeks. I can't go to bed every night worrying about it.

You spent some time on the State Investment Board. Can you tell me a little bit about it and what your role was?

The State Investment Board consists of 10 voting members, including one from the Senate, one from the House and the state treasurer. And they're responsible for investing billions of dollars of retirement money. When I was on there, the big economic drop came along and the state portfolio suffered. But I liked being on that. I didn't always go along with the majority. Sometimes, I wanted to put a little more money in savings and they didn't always want to go along with that.

How much stumping did you do for political hopefuls, either before your time in the Senate or during or after it?

I mainly supported a lot of members with cash contributions, and my name, whatever that was worth. I didn't get out and take a Saturday and go doorbell for them. I didn't have time, what with the business and legislative demands. But I'd go to fundraisers for them. I have bought $2,500 tables for Maria Cantwell and Patty Murray and gubernatorial candidates. Bette gets a little disgusted with me at times. I said, "We can afford it, we've had a lot of people help me." I can't back away from them. I'm going to be part of the action.

How about your campaigns? Were those mostly financed out of your pocket?

I had fundraisers, sure. A lot of people say you're foolish if you spend any of your own money. The first time I probably overdid it for the general.

I know you're not the type person who would want to do this, but I want you to define your legacy for me. The landmarks that bear your name are plentiful. There's a street in Long Beach, Sid's Market, the main spur leading into the Capitol of the largest state in the Pacific Northwest. There's a bench outside City Hall in Kelso; a bench at Lake Sacajawea in Longview; the port spur in Grays Harbor. What are your thoughts on all that, looking back?

Legacy is a pretty big word. Just like I mentioned names that I didn't expect you to remember. The real history buffs will go to the archives, go to Bette's book, go to your book and come up with some thoughts on what kind of a legacy I've left.

Are you satisfied with your life?

Oh, yeah. You know, my mother was a widow, and she thought a premier job was a job at Long-Bell or Weyerhaeuser. And I think I've accomplished a little more than that.

I'm sure your parents would be proud of you.

We're not just talking politics now. We're talking family. That is number one. I know in 1969, I think it was, we were at the National Legislative Conference in San Antonio. President Johnson was the main speaker, and I had an aisle seat. As he walked out, he stuck out his big paw and I stuck out mine. I got to shake hands with the president of the United States. I saw Harry Truman from the back of his train car when it went through Kelso. Those are the things you never forget. It's a shame that politicians don't have a better understanding of the other person. I read the other day [2012] that Congress' rating is down to 10 percent. *Ten percent*. But there's really more to that. When the pollsters ask, "What do you think of your own congressman?" it's a lot higher than that. I get worried about our country, I really do. We're eventually going to go over the cliff.

Were you always a dreamer?

I think I was.

Did you gain inspiration from your upbringing, your dreams, to help to propel you to the next level?

I think I had dreams. Family is the first one.

Where do you think you would have been if the elevator position had not opened up at the Capitol?

Well, I probably still would be living here in Long Beach. I may have ended up with the grocery store because Bud Underwood, the fellow that financed me, was still here.

You said before that if someone had held a gun to your head, you would have chosen groceries over politics.

Well …

Anything specific about the grocery business that tips the scale in that direction?

No. It's 51-49.

Spoken like a true politician.

Yep.

Snyder and Democratic Senator Lorraine Wojahn of Tacoma share a moment on the Senate floor in the 1990s. Wojahn, a pioneer whom Snyder believed was "one tough legislator," died one day before Snyder in October 2012. *Snyder family photo*

NOTES

One: Hell in a Handbasket

1. *Journal of the Senate: State of Washington*, Ninety-Seventh Day, April 19, 1997, p. 1711.

2. Ibid, pp. 1711-12.

3. Ibid., p. 1712.

4. Ibid., p. 1713.

5. Ibid.

6. Ibid., p. 1714.

Two: Little Chicago

1. McClary, Daryl C., "Allen Street (Kelso) Bridge collapses, with loss of life, on January 3, 1923," HistoryLink.org (http://www.historylink.org/index.cfm?DisplayPage=output.cfm&file_id=7406), August 3, 2005.

2. The United Press, "Victims Pinned Beneath Timbers in Wild Flood," *The Oakland Tribune*, January 4, 1923, p A3.

3. Ibid.

4. "Bridge With More Than 100 Persons on it Collapses, Feared Many are Dead," *The Helena Independent*, January 4, 1923, p. A1.

5. McClelland, John M. Jr., *R.A. Long's Planned City: The Story of Longview* (Longview, Washington: Longview Publishing Company, 1976), p. 116.

6. Bjorkman, Gewn Boyer, *The Descendants of Thomas Beeman of Kent, Connecticut: Assembled from the Beeman Genealogy by Clarence E. Beeman*, (Seattle, 1971), p. 2.

7. *An Illustrated History of North Idaho: Embracing Nez Perces, Idaho, Latah, Kootenai and Shoshone Counties* (State of Idaho: Western Historical Publishing Co., 1903), p. 256.

8. *An Illustrated History of Klickitat, Yakima and Kittitas Counties: With an Outline of the Early History of the State of Washington*, (Chicago: Interstate Publishing Company, 1904), p. 421.

9. Ibid.

10. Bjorkman, p. 84.

11. Ibid.

12. *An Illustrated History of North Idaho*, p. 256.

13. Andre Stepankowsky, "Historical museum to unveil extensive exhibit on flood of '33," *The Daily News*, May 15, 2008, http://tdn.com/lifestyles/historical-museum-to-unveil-extensive-exhibit-on-flood-of/article_73b13c64-47bd-56ee-a8af-doccf5388509.html (accessed June 12, 2012).

Three: Bette

1. Bette Snyder, *Politics Makes Strange Love Letters and Other Musings* (Self-published, May 2011), p. 242.

2. Ibid., p. 240.

3. Karen Bertroch, Donna Gatens-Klint, Jim LeMonds and Bryan Pentilla. *When Logging Was Logging: 100 Years of Big Timber in Southwest Washington*. (Virginia Beach, Virginia: The Donning Company, 2011), p. 132.

Four: Olympia Fever

1. Sharon Boswell, interviewer, *Ray Moore: An Oral History* (Olympia, Wash.: Washington State Oral History Program, Office of the Secretary of State, 1999), p. 28.

2. Bob Greive, "… from Olympia," *West Seattle Herald*, May 15, 1969, p. 9.

3. Daniel Jack Chasan, *Speaker of the House: The Political Career and Times of John L. O'Brien* (Seattle: University of Washington Press, 1990), pp. 103-104.

4. Gordon Walgren, *Gordon Walgren's Majority Leader's Cookbook* (self-published, 2004), p. 15.

5. Sharon Boswell, interviewer, *William Gissberg: An Oral History* (Olympia, Wash.: Washington State Oral History Program, Office of Secretary of State, 1996), p. 27.

6. Sharon Boswell, interviewer, *Elmer Huntley: An Oral History* (Olympia, Wash.: Washington State Oral History Program, Office of the Secretary of State, 1996), p. 49.

7. "Olympia Roundup," The *Arlington Times*, Jan. 17, 1963, p. 6.

8. "Little Girl Saved By Resuscitation Here Sun.," *The Chinook Observer*, November 3, 1961, p. A1.

Five: "A Portly Grocer"

1. Don Brazier, *History of the Washington Legislature: 1854-1963*, (Olympia: Washington State Senate, 2000), p. 162.

2. John C. Hughes, *Slade Gorton: A Half Century in Politics* (Olympia: Office of the Secretary of State, 2011), p. 49.

3. Anne Kilgannon, interviewer, *Joel M. Pritchard: An Oral History* (Olympia, Wash.: Washington State Oral History Program, Office of the Secretary of State, 2000), p. 150.

4. George A. Condon and Karl A. Van Asselt, "The Formation of a Coalition in the 1963 Washington State House of Representatives," from *Research Studies: A Quarterly Publication of Washington State University*, June 1966, p. 57.

5. The Associated Press, "Robert Bailey, longtime state legislator, dies in sleep at 87," *The Columbian*, Aug. 16, 2005, p. C4.

6. Daniel Jack Chasan, *Speaker of the House: The Political Career and Times of John L. O'Brien* (Seattle: University of Washington Press, 1990), p. 131.

7. Anne Kilgannon, interviewer, *Don Eldridge: An Oral History* (Olympia, Wash.: Washington State Oral History Program, Office of the Secretary of State, 2005), p. 412.

8. Leroy Hittle, "Jolly and Portly Grocer New House Chief Clerk," *The Walla Walla Union-Bulletin*, December 20, 1965, p. 5.

Six: Changing Chambers

1. Shelby Scates, "Angry Blacks Berate Solons In Eloquent Capitol Lecture," *Seattle Post-Intelligencer*, March 1, 1969, p. A2.

2. Don Brazier, *History of the Washington Legislature: 1854-1963*, (Olympia: Washington State Senate, 2007), p. 162.

3. David Postman, "Revered legislator Sid Snyder again tries retirement," *The Seattle Times*, November 23, 2002, http://community.seattletimes.nwsource.com/archive/?date=20021124&slug=sid24m (accessed on August 20, 2012).

4. Bette Snyder, *Politics Makes Strange Love Letters and Other Musings* (Self-published, May 2011), pp. 2-3.

5. Ibid., p. 63.

6. "Sid, Grocer of the Year," *Chinook Observer*, October 4, 1974, p. A1.

7. Adele Ferguson, "He's the only one laughing," *Tri-City Herald*, February 23, 1977, p. A6.

8.   James Wallace and Arthur C. Gorlick, "Gamscam: The case that broke the Democrats," *Seattle Post-Intelligencer*, September 14, 1989, p. A11.

Seven: Sedentary S.O.B.

1.   Doug Underwood, "Behind-scenes powerhouse may try for star Senate role," *The Seattle Times*, April 8, 1984, p. D5.

2.   Ibid.

3.   Sharon Boswell, interviewer, *August P. Mardesich: An Oral History*, (Olympia, Wash.: Washington State Oral History Program, Office of the Secretary of State, 2000), p. 45.

4.   The Associated Press, "Senate aide to stay on in deputy's post," *The Oregonian*, December 29, 1987.

5.   Bette Snyder, *Politics Makes Strange Love Letters and Other Musings* (Self-published, May 2011), p. 34.

6.   Ibid.

7.   Ibid.

8.   "Civility, compromise missing," *The Olympian*, March 18, 1998, p. A9.

9.   "The Observer recommends …," *The Chinook Observer*, September 12, 1990, p. A4.

10.   "Snyder's moxie is hard to beat," *The Daily World*, September 12, 1990, p. A4.

Eight: Senator

1.   Willard R. Espy, *Oysterville: Roads to Grandpa's Village*, (New York: C.N. Potter, 1974), p. 73

2.   Ibid.

3.   David Ammons, "Senate leader diagnosed with prostate cancer," *The Spokesman-Review*, January 9, 2002, p. B3.

4.   Mark Matassa and Jim Simon, "Capitol Asks: Where Are Leaders?" *The Seattle Times*, June 29, 1991, http://community.seattletimes.nwsource.com/archive/?date =19910630&slug=1291833 (accessed on June 12, 2012).

5.   Richard W. Larsen, "For Timber Towns, A Cry For Compassion," *The Seattle Times*, October 6, 1991, http://community.seattletimes.nwsource.com/archive/?da te=19911006&slug=1309395 (accessed August 12, 2012).

6.   The Associated Press, "Senate OKs measure to aid timber towns," *The Seattle Times*, March 21, 1991, http://community.seattletimes.nwsource.com/archive/?dat e=19910321&slug=1273107 (accessed August 12, 2012).

7. "Snyder tells concern for workers," *The Chinook Observer*, August 7, 1991, p. A1.

8. Bob Partlow, "Q&A: Sen. Sid Snyder," *The Olympian*, February 23, 1991, p. C3.

9. Hal Spencer, "State Senate Democrats enjoy picking majority leaders," *The Spokesman-Review*, November 13, 1992, p. B3.

10. David Postman and Robert Marshall Wells, "Session staggers to close: Democrats manhandle rules, Republicans to pass budget," *The News Tribune*, May 7, 1993, p. A1.

11. Ibid.

12. Ibid.

13. David Postman, "Legislature '94: Legislature plays 'Let's Make a Deal,'" *The News Tribune*, March 11, 1994, p. A7.

14. Helen Jung, "Despite Perks, Rural Wash. Is Hard Sell for Tech Firms," *The Wall Street Journal*, March 8, 2000, p. NW1.

15. Kathryn Robinson, "The Beltway's Worst Nightmare: A look at Linda Smith," *Seattle Weekly*, November 5, 1997, http://www.seattleweekly.com/1998-10-14/news/the-beltway-s-worst-nightmare/ (accessed September 1, 2012).

Nine: A Whim and a Prayer

1. David Postman, "Resignation No Whim, Says Town That Knows Sen. Sid Snyder Best," *The Seattle Times*, April 21, 1997, http://community.seattletimes.nwsource.com/archive/?date=19970421&slug=2535083 (accessed July 12, 2012).

2. "Sid Snyder's Civility," *The Seattle Times*, April 22, 1997, http://community.seattle-times.nwsource.com/archive/?date=19970422&slug=2535095 (accessed July 12, 2012).

3. Ibid.

4. Ibid.

5. *Journal of the Senate: State of Washington*, One-Hundred-Fourth Day, April 26, 1997, p. 2119.

6. Ibid.

7. Bill Hall, "Sid Snyder's sloppy decision to rejoin the Senate," *The Lewiston Tribune*, April 30, 1997, p. A10.

8. Bette Snyder, *Politics Makes Strange Love Letters and Other Musings* (Self-published, May 2011), p. 81.

9. Ibid., p. 82.

10. "Senate Resolution 1999-8677," *Journal of the Senate*, 1999, pp. 1,400-1401.

11. Mike Flynn, "Snyder exemplifies citizen legislator," *Puget Sound Business Journal*, April 23-29, 1999, pg. A3.

12. Sharon Boswell, interviewer, *Ray Moore: An Oral History* (Olympia, Wash.: Washington State Oral History Program, Office of the Secretary of State, 1999), p. 185.

13. Anne Kilgannon interviewer, "Sid Snyder's Capitol Stories: A Video Tour of the Legislative Buidling," Washington State Legislature's Oral History Program, 2002.

14. Bill Schumacher, "Bill Schumacher to run for Senate in 19th," July 2000 press release from Bill Schumacher, Washington Senate 2000 website http://web.archive. org/web/20020606023835/http://schumacher.nscteam.com/ (accessed July 12, 2012).

15. Joseph Turner, "Lawmaker apologizes for racially insensitive remark on Japanese," *The News Tribune*, September 19, 2001, p. B5.

16. David Ammons, "Senate Majority Leader Sid Snyder Diagnosed With Prostate Cancer," *Yakima Herald-Republic*, January 11, 2002, p. C2.

BIBLIOGRAPHY

Bertroch, Karen; Gatens-Klint, Donna; LeMonds, Jim and Pentilla, Bryan. *When Logging Was Logging: 100 Years of Big Timber in Southwest Washington*. Virginia Beach, Virginia: The Donning Company, 2011.

Bjorkman, Gwen Boyer. *The Descendants of Thomas Beeman of Kent, Connecticut: Assembled from the Beeman Genealogy by Clarence E. Beeman*. Seattle: Self-published, 1971.

Boswell, Sharon A. (interviewer). *William Gissberg: An Oral History*. Olympia, Washington: Washington State Oral History Program, 1996.

Boswell, Sharon A. (interviewer). *Elmer Huntley: An Oral History*. Olympia, Washington: Washington State Oral History Program, 1996.

Boswell, Sharon A. (interviewer). *Ray Moore: An Oral History*. Olympia, Washington: Washington State Oral History Program, 1999.

Boswell, Sharon A. (interviewer). *August P. Mardesich: An Oral History*. Olympia, Washington: Washington State Oral History Program, 2000.

Brazier, Don. *History of the Washington Legislature, 1854-1963*, Olympia: Washington State Senate, 2000.

Brazier, Don. *History of the Washington Legislature, 1965-1982*, Olympia: Washington State Senate, 2007.

Chasan, Daniel Jack. *Speaker of the House: The Political Career and Times of John L. O'Brien*. Seattle: University of Washington Press, 1990.

Condon, George A. and Van Asselt, Karl A. *The Formation of a Coalition in the 1963 Washington State House of Representatives*, from *Research Studies: A Quarterly Publication of Washington State University*, 1966.

Espy, Willard R. *Oysterville: Roads to Grandpa's Village*. New York: C.N. Potter, 1974.

Feagans, Raymond J. *The Railroad that Ran by the Tide*. Berkeley, California: Howell-North Books, 1972.

Hughes, John C. *Slade Gorton: A Half Century in Politics*. Olympia, Washington: Office of the Secretary of State, 2011.

Interstate Publishing Company. *An Illustrated History of Klickitat, Yakima and Kittitas Counties: With an Outline of the Early History of the State of Washington*. Chicago: Interstate Publishing Company, 1904.

Kilgannon, Anne (interviewer). *Don Eldridge: An Oral History*. Olympia, Washington: Washington State Oral History Program, 2005.

McClelland, John M. Jr. *R.A. Long's Planned City: The Story of Longview*. Longview, Washington: Longview Publishing Company, 1976.

Morgan, Murray. *Skid Road*. New York: The Viking Press, 1960.

Olsen, Mrs. Nels. *The Willapa Country History Report*. Raymond, Washington: *Raymond Herald & Advertiser*, 1965.

Seeberger, Edward D. *Sine Die: A Guide to the Washington State Legislative Process*. Seattle: University of Washington Press, 1997.

Snyder, Bette. *Politics Make Strange Love Letters and Other Musings*. Self-published, 2011.

Snyder, Bette and Snyder, Karen. *Crazy for Cranberries: The Everyday Cranberry Cookbook*. Self-published, 2002.

State of Idaho. *An Illustrated History of North Idaho: Embracing Nez Perces, Idaho, Latah, Kootenai and Shoshone Counties*. Idaho: Western Historical Publishing Co., 1903.

Strong, James Clark. *Biographical Sketch of James Clark Strong*. Los Gatos, Santa Clara County, California: Self-published, 1910.

Summers, Camilla G. *Kelso and Surrounding Area: 1820-1984*. Kelso, Washington: Summers Books, 1984.

Urrutia, Virginia. *They Came to Six Rivers: The Story of Cowlitz County*. Kelso, Washington: Cowlitz County Historical Society, 1998.

Walgren, Gordon. *Gordon Walgren's Majority Leader's Cookbook*. Self-published, 2004.

ACKNOWLEDGEMENTS

Work to preserve Sid Snyder's incredible story for posterity began in 2006 when Sharon A. Boswell conducted a series of interviews with Snyder for the state's Legislative Oral History Project. The project languished for a few years until it was revived in 2011 by a group of Snyder's closest friends and family, and I was brought on board to finish the work of documenting Snyder's many legendary stories and also to write a comprehensive biography of the man adored by so many. During that process, I came to adore a few people as well. First and foremost were Sid and Bette Snyder and their family. I could not have asked for a better group of people to spend the snow- and sun-filled year with. To paraphrase Sid: It was always nice at the beach.

Others to whom I owe gratitude include (with apologies to those I may have missed): Randy and Judy Anderson, Rick Anderson, Louie Balukoff, Doug Barker, Stu Beitler, Sharon A. Boswell, Don Brazier, Jim Bricker, Chris Britt, Marty Brown, Andrew Burlingame, Grayson Burlingame, Kathy Campbell, Maria Cantwell, Scott Chisa, Ethan Chung, Carol Coulter, *Chinook Observer*, Cole Cosgrove, Lee and Melinda Crowley, Aaron Dean, Jane Doumit, Mark Doumit, Milt Doumit, Bruce Drysdale, Pat Dunn, Susan Dunn, Kirsten Erwin, Dan Evans, Steve Excell, Lauren Foster, Steven Friederich, Jane Goldberg, Slade Gorton, Chris Gregoire, Dan Grimm, Bob Hamilton, Brian Hatfield, Trova Heffernan, Tom Hoemann, Kevin Hong, John C. Hughes, Patsy Hughes, Carleen Jackson, Vickie Jenkins, Anne Kilgannon, Erik Kupka, Ellen Landino, Barbara LaBoe, Lori Larson, Peter Lewis, Dan McDonald, Sally McNulty, Malcolm and Ardell McPhail, Steve McPhail, Danielle Meeker, Laura Mott, Jonathan Nesvig, *Pacific County Press*, Kim Patten, Lisa Patterson, Tierney Patterson, Ray Paxton, Sally Paxton, Drew Perine, Kathy Quigg, Sam Reed, Jan Richardson, Jeannine Roe, Ben Rosenthal, *The Seattle Times*, *Seattle Post-Intelligencer*, Dee Anne Shaw, Azmi and Florence Shawa, Nabiel Shawa, Karen Snyder, Sid Snyder Jr., John Spellman, Sydney Stevens, *The Daily News*, *The Daily World*, *The News Tribune*, TVW, Max Vekich, Gordon Walgren, Dave Wilkins, *Willapa Harbor Herald*, Barb Winkler, Vickie Winters, and Nyla Wood.

DONORS

David and Kathy Aase

James Andersen

Robert and Judith Andrew

Craig Apperson and Leslie Goldstein

Sherry Appleton

Dick Armstrong

Association of Washington Business

Lynn and Rolf Ausen

Clyde and Ruth Ballard

Rick and Donna Ballard

Bank of the Pacific

Al and Margaret Bauer

Jennifer Belcher

Jerry Benning

Duane Berentson

John Betrozoff

Rebecca Bogard

Kathleen Boyle

Julie Brandsness

Jim Bricker

Ross Briggs

Marge Brouillet

Mark and Julia Brown

Marty and Kate Brown

Max and Shannon Brown

Sam Brown

Kandy Kink Bruesch

David and Becky Buri

Judy Burns and Jerry Ellis

David Campiche and Laurie Anderson

Jon and Joan Chambreau

Mary Chaney

Judith A. Childs

Frank Chopp Jr. and Nancy Long

Mike and Carol (Monohon) Conley

Fred and Pat Cook

Tony and Joy Cook

Carol and Tim Coulter

Cowlitz County Democrats

Frankie and W.O. Crain

Ron and Wanda Crockett

Lee and Melinda Crowley

Bud and Jean Cuffel

Julie Culbertson

Lucille Deccio

Democratic Club of Cowlitz County

Norm and Suzie Dicks

Robin Donohue

Mark Doumit

Katherine Dunn

Patrick and Susan Dunn

Dwight Eager

H. Stuart Elway

John and Susan Evans

Steve Excell

Darlene Fairley

Muriel (Sandison) Faunce

Roy and Connie Ferguson

Fred Finn

Lee and Shirley Fisher

Dennis Fleenor

Dean and Sharon Foster

Connie Freeland

Senator Georgia Gardner

Bill Garvin

Marc and Scott Gaspard

Jim and Virginia Gately

Dave Geddes

Rosalie Gittings

Carolyn and Guy Glenn

Lynne Glore

Kathleen and Dave Glose

Douglas and Mary Goelz

Slade and Sally Gorton

Donna Graham

Karen and Steve Gray

Eugene and Marjorie Green

Don and Reema Griffith

Milt and Sarah Gudgell

Duane and Sharon Hagstrom

Pat and Bob Hall

Jerry Harper

Jeff and Casey Harrell

Ron and Karen Harrell

Rich Hartman

Robert and Genevieve Hatfield

Mary Margaret Haugen and Basil Badley

Joyce Hawkins

Michael Heavey

Denny and Paula Heck

Brad Hendrickson and Laura McDowell

Lorraine and William Hine

Randy and Tina Hodgins

Tom and Lee Hoemann

Barbara B. Howard

Glen Hudson

John and Patsy Hughes

Paul and Lucy Isaki

Jerry and Wanda Jackson

Bill and Patricia Jacobs

Rachel and Ken Jacobsen

Eric D. Johnson

Melissa R. Johnson and Matt Brown

Jim and Suzi Justin

Ruth Kagi

Dean and Cathy Kary

Frank L. Keller

Robert E. Kelly

James L. Kennedy

Lynn and Keith Kessler

Ed and Catherine Ketel

Eric and Sara Kirschenman

Tony and Ann Kischner

James Kneeland

Roger and Nancy Krause

Becky Larsen

Thomas and Susan Lavack

Charlotte Lawrence

Jean Leonard and Bill Grabb

Mark and Claire Litchman

Gary and Mona Locke

Dennis and Kathy Long

John Lovick

A. Pierre Marchand

Dick and Elizabeth Marquardt

Jonathan and Andrea Mayner

Mark and Theresa McCrady

Malcolm and Ardell McPhail

Scott and Kim Merriman

Microsoft Corporation

Cherri and Greg Miles

Louise and Stafford Miller

Victor and Patti Moore

Ralph Moore and Barb Phillips

Buddy and Terry Moreman Jr.

Patricia Durham Morton

Richard Munsen, M.D.

Tom and Laurie Napa

Mrs. John L. O'Brien

Mike O'Connell

Sen. Gary and Kathleen Odegaard

Valeria and Daniel Ogden

Nancey Olson

Steve Oman

Angela Owens

Pacific County Democrats

Timothy J. and Marsha Parker

Cole Paxton

Jack Paxton

Sally and Ray Paxton

Peninsula Sanitation/Jay Alexander and Diane Carter

Bob and Toshie Petersen

Donald and Norma Petersen

Nancy Peterson

Adele Ferguson Philipsen

Lucille Pierce

William and Margaret Pound

Margarita Prentice

Jack Preston

David Quall

Bruce Reeves

Phil Rockefeller

Dave Rodgers

Charles and Marilyn Roe

Jeannine Roe

Rich and Karen Rollman

Betty and Ron Rosevear

Polly Rosmond

Richard and Nancy Rust

Sabey Corporation

Derek Sandison

Robert and Sally Schaefer

Shannon Schaeffer

Gene Schlatter

K. Gordon Schoewe

Gordon Schultz

David Schumacher and Katy Johansson

George W. Scott

Seattle Mariners

Peggy Shanahan

Nabiel Shawa

Brian and Marilyn Sheldon

Richard and Ruth Sheldon

James and Janice Shipman

Adam and Sara Smith

Monte Snider

Robert and Jane Snow

Calvin Snyder and Selamawit Gebrekidan

James Snyder

Karen Snyder and Bob Hamilton

Sid Snyder Jr. and Robin Powell

Whitney Snyder

Helen Sommers

Harriet Spanel

Gayle and Gunars Sreibers

Frank Stagen

Melanie Stewart

Marilyn Stormans

Marvin and Judy Stutzman

Darilyn Sundstrom

Charlene and F. R. Sutherland

Al and Paula Swift

Philip, Darlene and Matthew Talmadge

Scott and Charlotte Taylor

John and Elizabeth Terrey

Pat Thibaudeau

Alan and Barbara Thompson

Bob Thompson

Earl and Barbara Tilly

Frances and Clifford Traisman

Harry and Sheryl Trask

Tom and Darcel Troy

Tom and Judy Troy

Bob and Elizabeth Uttter

Georgette Valle

Richard Van Wagenen

Craig Voegele

Gordon and Sue Walgren

Judy and Roy Warnick

Beverly Warnke

Shirley and Jack Wayland

Roger and Nina Weld

Rick and Claudia Wickman

Gustave and Lila Wiegardt Jr.

Janet Wilson

Robbyn Wilson

Charles and Angella Winn

Shirley Winsley

Vickie Winters

Brian and Eileen Wirkkala

Maggie Wolstenholme

Deryl and Nyla Wood

Mike Woodin and Amy Bell

Dale Woods

Jim and Joy Zorn

Washington Federation of State Employees

Washington Food Industry Association

Washington Forest Protection Association

INDEX

ABOUT THE AUTHOR

Jeff Burlingame is the Image Award-winning author of more than twenty nonfiction books. His work has been honored by the New York Public Library and the NAACP, which in 2012 awarded him its highest literary honor, an Image Award, during a nationally televised event in Los Angeles. The previous year, he also was one of five Image Award finalists—along with eventual winner, former Secretary of State Condoleezza Rice—and attended the Los Angeles ceremony. Prior to becoming an author, Burlingame spent more than a dozen years in print media and won several awards from the Society of Professional Journalists during that time.